The Friendship Book

A THOUGHT FOR EACH DAY | **2019**

The Friendship Book

WE'VE started on a journey, Lord,
A journey through the year,
And who knows just what lies ahead?
We pray the way is clear.
We bring you all our hopes and dreams,
Those wishes deep within,
We ask for courage and for strength
To see each day begin.
We send out love and healing thoughts
To those in distant lands,
Where there is turmoil may they find
The gift of caring hands.
We thank you for companionship
And all each day can bring,
The comfort found in love and faith
They help our spirits sing.
And so once more we ask you, Lord,
Please be our guard and guide,
And on our journey through the year
Be always by our side.

– Iris Hesselden.

January

IT'S a tradition in some places to clean the house in preparation for the New Year. Harry told me he thought that sort of thing was best left until the spring. So I asked him what he did instead.

It seems he takes a notebook and walks through the various rooms and his garden, trying to see them all with a new eye, noting what needs repaired, wondering what might be improved, and considering what might be put to better use.

"Usually there is enough there to keep me busy for the rest of the year," he said. "And, having done that, I sit down with some ginger wine and shortbread, and look at myself in the same way. There's generally plenty of work needing doing there as well!"

It's all too easy to get complacent, whether it be with the place we live or with how we live. New Year is the time for all sorts of new beginnings. May the changes be only good ones for you and yours in the year ahead.

Now, I hope Harry has saved me some ginger wine!

Wednesday — January 2

WE tend to make New Year's resolutions about earthly things, believing they affect our lives more directly. Imagine we raised our sights a little. What difference might that make?

Jonathan Edwards, an 18th-century clergyman, wrote, "Resolution One – I will live for God. Resolution Two – even if no-one else does, I still will."

Let's resolve to focus, as best we can, on heavenly matters this year, and see how those earthly concerns are taken care of in passing.

Thursday — January 3

A FRIEND is someone that you choose,
And pick from all the rest.
A friend is someone that you know
Will always do their best
To pick you up, and walk with you,
Through times when you feel sad,
To celebrate when times are good,
And truly show they're glad.
A friend is someone you can trust,
Someone who's kind and true,
A friend can turn the day around,
When you are feeling blue.
So if you have a friend like that,
Just stop and take the time
To say, "You're such a special friend,
And I'm so glad you're mine."

– Linda Brown.

Friday — January 4

HER voice is like water on leather," someone said. I'd never heard the expression before, so I looked it up.

When leather gets wet the oils that keep it supple get lifted to the surface and washed away, so the leather becomes less flexible and it cracks more easily. In other words, by constantly complaining the woman in question was really making her own life worse.

A legitimate complaint is a fine thing, but sometimes complaining becomes a default position; we do it for attention, and we end up driving people away. So fewer people are willing to help us. Then we feel we have more to complain about! And so on.

But wet leather can be restored if the damage is caught soon enough. By the reapplication of oils the old softness can be recaptured.

All very informative, I suppose. But useful? Only in as much as it encourages me to ask the question, will the words I speak today be like water on leather – or more like the restoring oils?

Scenic grandeur.

Harrop Tarn, Lake District.

Saturday — January 5

WARREN had been called to do carpentry work at a very nice, very expensive, house. Arriving a little early, he took a walk around the gardens, where he met a man who introduced himself as the head gardener. They chatted for a while about gardens in the winter, and the work Warren was going to be doing.

"You may be the head gardener," Warren said, "but are you also the home-owner?"

It turned out his hunch was right and he mentally reran their entire conversation to see if he had said anything disrespectful to the man who, as it turned out, would be paying his wages. Thankfully, he had been nothing but interested and courteous.

When he told me that, I laughed. But then I wondered . . .

What if the people I meet are my "home-owner" in disguise: God, or His much-loved children? What if He is there, listening when we talk?

Would I have a clear conscience, like Warren? How much would I wish I hadn't said?

It's a powerful thought. One that encourages me to try to do better!

Sunday — January 6

HENRY JAMES was talking about writing to other writers when he said, "We work in the dark, we do what we can, we give what we have. Our doubt is our passion and our passion is our task."

But, given how our best efforts at doing good often work out in such surprising ways, with results we could never have anticipated when we first began, he might as well have been talking about the life of faith and service.

His one complaint was that writers spent their lives perfecting their art, but sadly, they had no second time around to put what they learned into practice. For those of us working in the dark of this world, doing what we can, giving what we have, there is, thankfully, another life waiting where we will understand more clearly, and more joyfully, how it all worked out.

Monday — January 7

OUR dear friend Mary has been taking computer lessons, and was delighted to show us the new laptop she bought.

Mostly, she intends to use it to keep in touch with family living abroad, but she also plans to write her memoirs – which should be fascinating!

Right now, she is just having fun playing with it. She called up a page to write something on.

"Watch this!" she said. She moved the cursor to one part of the page and a menu popped up. She moved it to the other side of the screen and a "scroll bar" appeared.

"But when you aren't actually in those places," she said, "you have no idea anything is there! It's just like that old saying about not judging someone until you have walked in their shoes. Unless you are actually there, you have no idea what's really going on."

Ah, Mary. No matter how modern her life gets, she will always find the old-fashioned wisdom in it!

Tuesday — January 8

I READ a book by a man who toured Yorkshire on foot, bus and horse-drawn cart. In it he recounted the kindnesses of the people he met.

Inside the volume, perhaps as a bookmark, was a bus ticket from one of the routes the author had taken, dated ten years later (and still half a century ago).

Did that reader, I wondered, meet similarly inspirational characters along the way, or did he look around and think people must have been nicer back then?

Time wouldn't have make the difference. Or the bus route.

What, I guess, might have made a difference was the kind of people the author and the reader expected to meet on their different but similar travels.

Expect to be delighted, say I. And your journeys will be much more interesting!

Wednesday — January 9

WOULD you like to go on a spiritual pilgrimage, perhaps to some fabled shrine?

The German writer Herman Hesse wrote of such a thing in his book "Journey To The East". But his travellers never reached their destination. They disbanded wearily, and returned home frustrated – only to find their lessons in grace awaiting them in their own towns, and each of their homes was the shrine they sought.

By all means, travel far abroad. But if it's a spiritual journey you want to go on, begin and end wherever you happen to be. All of the lessons, and all of the achievements, will be right there, waiting for you.

Thursday — January 10

GREAT-AUNT LOUISA records that she once shared her diary with a close friend.

"Why do you write about such relentlessly cheerful subjects, when there is so much that is difficult in life?" her friend asked.

Louisa laughed it off at the time, but later, she wrote, "I do not deny that this world has a plentiful supply of hard toil and worries. And I feel it only right that I also address those issues – once I have finished writing about all the good I can find in an ordinary life. That, however, might take some considerable time."

As far as we know, she never did get around to it.

Friday — January 11

THOSE who manage woodlands will, from time to time, deliberately leave piles of logs or branches on the ground among the trees. They look like they have simply been stacked and forgotten. But they provide shelter for small creatures, food for insects and, ultimately, they refresh the soil from which they came.

How wonderful would it be to live a life in which even the things we leave lying around served a useful purpose?

Life in the forest.

Saturday — January 12

WHILE the year is still young, we could do worse than think a while on these words by Anne Frank:

"How noble and good everyone could be if, every evening before falling asleep, they were to recall to their minds the events of the whole day and consider exactly what had been good or bad. Then, without realising it, you start to improve yourself at the start of each new day."

Imagine, if we did, how noble and good we could be by this time next year!

Sunday — January 13

FRANCES HODGSON BURNETT, who wrote the children's classic "The Secret Garden", said, "If you look the right way, you can see the whole world is a garden."

We might have to squint more in some places than in others, but it's nonetheless true. Perhaps learning to look at this world, and this life, and see them as the precious gifts from God they truly are is the real secret.

Monday — January 14

ONE of the most inspirational characters in Victor Hugo's novel "Les Misérables" is Bishop Myriel who gave Jean Valjean the chance to start again.

He was based on a real-life cleric from the same area whose nickname was Monseigneur Bienvenu – Father Welcome. He acquired the title from his characteristically effusive greetings and the genuine warmth of his hospitality.

It's a lovely notion, and it started me wondering. If we were each to be known by our most notable characteristic, or how we related to others, would we be happy, or would we then be *les misérables*?

I imagine most of us would be pleased, but those who weren't could always do what Jean Valjean did, and start again!

Tuesday — January 15

THE soul. We all have one. But who can say for sure what it is, how it is shaped, whether it may be affected by earthly things? The Roman philosopher Marcus Aurelius strongly believed that "The soul becomes dyed with the colour of its thoughts."

Spend a moment in idle speculation with me, if you will, and consider the idea. Do you tend towards more serious thoughts, or more joyful? Flighty? Complex? If your thoughts really did colour your soul, would it be blue, magenta, orange or slate-grey?

Personally, I rather hope mine is tie-dyed!

Wednesday — January 16

ROBERT HENRI once said, "There is a joy in the pursuit of anything." I think back to the times I physically chased anything – a fellow racer, a kite, a dog. When the limbs are working, when the heart is pumping, that is indeed joyful.

But if we are pursuing, something must be chased. It isn't always fun for them.

Perhaps I can recommend the deeper joy of waiting, trusting your needs will be met, and knowing also that whatever comes willingly to you was meant to be with you.

Thursday — January 17

IT was an overheard conversation between two young men. One was paint-splattered and had obviously been doing someone a good deed. His friend couldn't understand why when there was nothing in it for him.

The painted fellow considered his response, then said, "Maybe because I was born the right height to reach the top of the walls without a stepladder. And I don't have arthritis in my spine like he does, so I can reach the bottom as well."

I am sure that young man knows a lot about counting his blessings, and he could teach his friend about the fine art of appreciating them.

Friday — January 18

FIND meaning! Isn't that what humankind has been trying to do throughout the ages? Cults have grown up around it, businesses have tried to supply it through material goods. Some find it in kindness, worship or love.

I did have to smile at the suggestion of the philosopher and writer Albert Camus, who said, "Find meaning . . . Go out for a walk."

Why did I smile?

Because sometimes going for a walk and being reminded that we are part of a greater Creation is all the meaning we ever need.

Saturday — January 19

THERE is a description of the Apostle Paul that says he was "small of stature, balding, bow legs, large eyes, eyebrows meeting, nose slightly hooked – yet his appearance was full of grace: sometimes he looked more like an angel than a man."

That's quite some transformation!

If you are looking to live your life by a faith or a philosophy (and I do recommend it), make sure it is one that brings out the very best of you.

Sunday — January 20

HAVE you ever seen those "Where's Wally" books? Each double-page spread is crammed full of characters, animals and equipment. There's always a lot going on.

And the task is to find one person – Wally – in the midst of it all. It's not easy, but the one reassurance is that he's always there, somewhere!

The year ahead will be full of distractions. Our days might become quite crowded. Try always to find God in the crowd.

I mean no disrespect in comparing God to a character created to amuse children, but there is one similarity, one reassurance. Like Wally, God will always be there, somewhere!

Monday — January 21

*O*N *my stile I sit and ponder,*
Rippling waters trickling by,
Home and village nestling yonder,
Verdant lea, azure the sky.
Lilting birdsong all around me
Charms my mind, delight to hear.
What more might any mystic see,
Than here and now, God's gifts so dear?
Who needs power, glory, wealth
When I share gems such as these?
Add sight and sense, pray good health,
Thank you, Nature; bless me, please!

– George Hughes.

Tuesday — January 22

SHERLOCK HOLMES, in the books at least, was always right, no matter how outlandish his predictions. But the 2015 movie "Mr Holmes" focused on a mistake. Holmes, touchingly portrayed by Sir Ian McKellen, is haunted by a time when being right was the most important thing for him.

A powerful lesson is learned, one that has been explained many ways. It comes down to this — if we need to choose between being right and being kind, always be kind. We will be right!

Wednesday — January 23

IT'S amazing what can help in a difficult situation. The Lady of the House often tells me I am wearing my mouth the wrong way to get something done. She means it would be easier if I smiled. And the American poet Edgar Guest suggested something similar.

"He started to sing as he tackled the thing
That couldn't be done – and he did it!"

A smile, a song – two ways we can make difficult situations easier for ourselves.

Thursday — January 24

SHE came into some unexpected money and assured me she would pay me back at last. But then she wanted to make a confession.

"I conned you that time," she said. "I didn't need the money. I just made up an excuse to see if you would give it to me."

"I knew that," I now confessed. "But I also knew you needed someone in your life who trusted you."

"I felt so bad about that for so long. In fact, I felt so bad I gave up conning people so I wouldn't have to feel that way again."

"Then I've been paid back already," I said.

Friday — January 25

ROBERT BURNS, whose poetry and life we celebrate today, was a man of passions.

In later years, when many passions die down, he did indeed produce fewer poems. But that might have been because he was travelling the country collecting folk songs.

He loved to join in with a good sing-song, even though his voice was apparently less than melodious. But he still sang!

In Robert Burns's honour, let's celebrate this day, and this life, with whatever talents we have, but mostly with passion!

Saturday — January 26

WATCHING "Bambi" (for the umpteenth time) with a little one, it occurred to me that we hear a lot from Thumper's father, despite him never actually making an appearance. Mother Rabbit repeatedly asks, "Thumper, what did your father say?" Then the little rabbit repeats his father's words of wisdom.

Of course, Mr Rabbit didn't come up with all that wisdom by himself. He had writers to help him! But, still, almost eighty years later, children hear that advice on families sticking together, only saying nice things, and always eating your greens.

May we use our words as wisely, and to such long-lasting effect.

THANK you, Lord, for bringing me
So safely through the night,
Through all the hours of darkness
Until the morning light.
Forgive me when I toss and turn
And sleep is hard to find,
I know I should depend on you
To give me peace of mind.
But just sometimes a troubled day
Can leave a troubled soul,
The problems all come crowding in
And often take their toll.
So be with me through every night
And guide me through the day,
Reminding me each moment, Lord,
You're never far away.

– Iris Hesselden.

Monday — January 28

IN 1935 writer and educator M.V. O'Shea compiled a book of children's stories called "Eyes And No Eyes And Other Stories". The title story is of two boys returning to school after a cross-country walk.

Asked about the walk by a teacher, Robert declared it had been boring and nothing worthy of his attention had occurred. The time spent walking had, as far as he was concerned, been wasted.

William, who arrived later, had tales of a brightly coloured woodpecker, a peat-cutter who showed him a grass snake, the view from a windmill, an otter and a heron in the river, a clump of marl encrusted with sea-shells, and the size of the moon as it rose above the horizon, signalling it was time to head back.

The teacher tells the boys, "The observing eye and enquiring mind will find matter for improvement and delight in every ramble, in town or country. Do you, then, William continue to make use of your eyes; and you, Robert, learn that eyes were given you to use."

Tuesday — January 29

THE past year had been difficult for both men. The year coming showed no signs of being better.

"But I expect it shall have flowers," one said. "Because I've already planted the seeds."

There will be powers at play this year over which we have no control, but we have a bigger say in our happiness, and the happiness of others, than many imagine.

If you wish tomorrow to be brighter, smell more fragrant, bring more joy, then start planting today!

Wednesday — January 30

TOM is a regular fount of folk-wisdom. In the recent cold spell he has been advising friends to leave a tap dripping overnight. The water in the pipes wouldn't be sitting still and would be less likely to freeze.

Tom obviously doesn't have a water meter! But wouldn't that be a great way to treat a friendship that had gone cold? Keep the kind words, the occasional note, any little contact you can imagine dripping away so things don't freeze over completely.

That way the friendship will still be in some sort of working order when the thaw comes and warmer relations can be resumed.

Maybe Tom isn't such a drip after all!

Thursday — January 31

A WISE man was asked the secret of a good life. He told the seeker to open his hands. "What can you do with them?" he asked.

"I can scoop up water, I can caress a cheek, I can give a gift, I can wave to a friend . . ."

"Now close your hands and tell me what you can do."

"I can hide things, I can strike, I can inspire fear."

The wise man nodded. "A good life is lived with open hands."

Planting seeds.

February

THE American writer Leo Rosten once wrote, "I think the purpose of life is . . . to matter, to count, to stand for something, to have it made some difference that you lived at all."

And I agree!

So, how do we do that? We don't need to make a big splash on the world stage. In fact, we might do it without ever achieving any level of fame whatsoever. We make a difference when we teach a child that life is good, when we show someone they are not alone, when we offer a second chance or a word of encouragement.

There are, of course, other, more negative, ways to make a difference, but only love, in its many different guises, moves life forward.

So, in short, in my humble opinion, the purpose of life is to love!

Saturday — February 2

I WAS reminded of a beautiful hymn today – by a crocodile! A walking crocodile is what the local nursery calls it when they take the pre-schoolers to the park. Each child holds a loop on a brightly coloured nylon strap, meaning everyone is connected.

The nursery teacher told them to walk at a steady pace and in the same direction, so no-one would be pulled off their feet. When one boy kept letting go of his loop, a girl put her hand through her loop and took his hand, so they were all still joined together.

In the 18th century Gerhard Tersteegan wrote:

"Come, children, let us go. We travel hand in hand.
Each in his brother finds his joy, in this wild stranger land.
As children let us be, nor by the way fall out.
The angels guard us, round about, and help us brotherly.
Let the strong be quick to raise the weaker when they fall.
Let love and peace and patience bloom in ready help for all."

Sunday — February 3

WHEN we take lessons, it's good to learn from an expert. So, learning about art from Vincent van Gogh would be ideal – if he was still around! He can't show us how to prepare a canvas, mix paint or see the magic in a starry night. But he left these words: "I feel that there is nothing more truly artistic than to love people."

Monday — February 4

I WAS just about to start another daily chore
When a swift glance through the window sent me running
* to the door.*
Spanning roofs and high brick walls, away beyond my view,
A rainbow shimmered colours of every shade and hue.
I couldn't help but stand there – I couldn't bear to miss
The glory of this moment, as nature reached to kiss
My mundane Monday morning with a sign from God above,
That between life's sun and rain we have the promise of His love.
I watched my lovely rainbow slowly disappear from sight,
But caught within the heart are those which shine for ever bright
The kindness of a stranger or the love of a dear friend
Sent in your time of need – a rainbow without end!

– Marion Cleworth.

Tuesday — February 5

FEBRUARY is generally a winter month, seen by some as the time to start preparing for spring. The name of the month comes from the Latin word "Februa" which means "to purify".

It is quite appropriate for the time of year; a time when we might clear the debris of winter away and prepare the ground for the green shoots that will soon make an appearance.

It might also be a philosophy to apply to the difficult times in life. When things have been cold and dark for long enough, find your own emotional February, purify your heart and situation, then wait and watch for the green shoots of recovery.

Wednesday — February 6

TIME and again I hear great mysteries explained simply and great truths explained in a few words. It was an overheard conversation on an Edinburgh street. The little girl must have been about three years old.

"Grampa," she asked, "why did you help a stranger you didn't even know?"

Grampa seemed, for a moment, to search for a better explanation. Then he settled for, "Because he needed help."

Simple enough to stay in a child's mind. Powerful enough, I have no doubt, to shape that child's life. Well done, Grampa!

Thursday — February 7

I SUPPOSE the modern online equivalent would be Pinterest, or some such. But I do have a soft spot for the old-style Commonplace Book (sometimes referred to as a Hodgepodge Book).

It might be likened to a diary, but it was more like a scrapbook, and would vary according to the interests of the owner. The book would be there when its owner wanted to note down something that caught his or her interest, be it recipes, songs, advice . . .

A friend of mine uses hers to take notes on moments of grace.

There is much that is worth recording in the commonplace. And a well-kept Commonplace Book means we get to share them with others or simply enjoy them ourselves, again and again, long after the moment itself has passed.

Friday — February 8

WHAT would make you happy?
The great writer Oscar Wilde drew up a short list. It consisted of "freedom, books, flowers, and the moon."

Draw up your own list.

You will be surprised how many of the things on it are close at hand or free for you to enjoy.

A quiet corner in Scotland's capital.

Circus Lane in Stockbridge, Edinburgh.

Saturday — February 9

MINDFULNESS and "being in the moment" have enjoyed a resurgence in popularity in recent years. But it's no new concept, as demonstrated by these words from the poet Henry Wadsworth Longfellow.

"For, after all, the best thing one can do when it is raining, is to let it rain."

The beauty in a shower of rain is something we might all benefit from being mindful of.

Sunday — February 10

MODERN architects have an astounding variety of building materials: roof tiles that convert sunlight into electricity, glass that changes from opaque to transparent. But they don't compare with art critic John Ruskin's idea of a perfect building material.

"What fairy palaces we may build of beautiful thought . . . treasure-houses of precious and restful thoughts which care cannot disturb, nor pain make gloomy."

And unlike all the rest, beautiful thoughts are absolutely free!

Monday — February 11

I HAVE four "quarter-days" in my calendar (this is one). On each of those days I rise a little earlier and take a walk across the fields and through the woods.

Why? Because I am attempting to rise to a challenge from over three centuries ago. The poet and clergyman Thomas Traherne wrote that we fail to enjoy this world properly "till every morning you awake in heaven; see yourself in your Father's palace and look upon the skies, the earth and the air as celestial joys; having such a reverend esteem of all as if you were among the angels."

I do OK in spring, summer and autumn – even outside my quarter-days – but our northern climate means I struggle with seeing heaven in the rain and the wind. But I shall persevere. You see, I am determined to enjoy this world properly.

Tuesday — February 12

I KNOW not who penned the lines, but they made me think. "Love ever gives, forgives, outlives, and ever stands with open hands. And while it lives, it gives. For this is love's prerogative; to give and give and give."

Hmm, I thought, a little cynically perhaps, and what happens when you run out of whatever it is you might be giving in love?

Then I heard a laugh at the back of my mind and a soft voice asked, "Have you ever known it to happen?"

No, I had to admit, I never have.

Wednesday — February 13

WHEN the days are bleak and wintry, we might turn to the poet William Wordsworth for a little comfort.

"There is a blessing in the air," he wrote, "which seems a sense of joy to yield to the bare trees, and mountains bare, and grass in the green field."

Are you feeling the blessing? The sense of joy? Keep looking. It may be something we discover, or it may be that in seeking it we create it. But Mr Wordsworth would not deceive us. It is out there.

Thursday — February 14

THE joy of spring pervades the air,
Sweet life renewing everywhere!
Lambs a-leaping in the leas
And catkins forming on the trees.
Celandines, delight to see
On slender stems that shine for me.
Primroses nestled on the bank
Remind me my dear Lord to thank,
For all these gifts of life He sends
Each, every year when winter ends!

– George Hughes.

27

A granddaughter's hug.

Friday — February 15

PEOPLE are happy to tell you what they think of the world – often at great length. In their minds, they will simply be stating the facts.

But I wonder how those "facts" might be altered if we could preface such discussions with these words by Ralph Waldo Emerson – "People do not seem to realise that their opinion of the world is also a confession of their character."

The world is what it is, but how we see it depends on how we look, what we focus on, and what we expect to see.

How's your world looking today?

Saturday — February 16

THERE were journeys beginning, moving on to the next leg, or ending, in the main concourse of that airport. Everyone seemed very busy, very focused.

Then there was a squeal and a three-year-old ran right into the midst of it all. Her grandad told me he panicked, thinking she might fall over a suitcase, or that someone might trip over her. People wouldn't be happy!

But everyone stopped in their tracks, letting her pass, and everyone smiled when she reached her grandmother (who had been away for a fortnight).

There were a lot of important journeys taking place there at that time, but everyone seemed to agree that there aren't many journeys more important than the one that takes a little girl to her gran.

Sunday — February 17

THE great Russian novelist Dostoyevsky wrote, "The soul is healed by being with children."

The other day, in church, a two-year-old I barely know reached for me. I lifted him. He put his arms around my neck, rested his curls against my cheek, and he hugged me tightly.

My soul was healed, my heart overflowed. It was like God Himself had sent the hug.

Monday — February 18

LEO was looking around for his wife. I met him at the door, and we fell to discussing one of the big differences between the sexes, and a big question of faith.

Knowing they had been through a difficult time recently, I said it was nice to see the family looking so happy and, by the way, that was one grace-filled wife he had.

"I know." He sighed. "Too grace-filled sometimes. Every time someone does something wrong she's nice to them, and nice about them, always trying to see their point of view. Whereas, if I think they are wrong, I want to do something about it."

"It's a man thing," I agreed. "We always want to fix things. But the ladies just want to let it go, get on, and wait for God to fix it."

"And she does the same to me! If I'm wrong, I'd rather be told I'm wrong, but no, she brushes it aside and keeps on loving me!"

"The Lady of the House does the same!" I said. "Why can't they just listen to us?"

Leo laughed in what seemed, for a second, like agreement.

"Because we're wrong?"

Are our wives, and others like them, too grace-filled? Only by the standards of those of us who need to be more grace-filled.

Tuesday — February 19

THESE days we tend to live lives that are fairly sheltered from the elements – which is nice if you want to stay cosy! But, every once in a while, I do feel we need to connect with the outside world for the good of our soul. I imagine the early 20th-century novelist and designer Edith Wharton felt something similar when she wrote, "Set wide the window. Let me drink the day."

Don't just do it on sunny days. Enjoy all the different faces the weather has to show you.

On the wilder days, drink it in, for a moment, then close the window again. You will feel ever so much more cosy for having done so!

Wednesday — February 20

WE all feel a little low from time to time. So, perhaps we ought to take the advice of the Queen of Dollywood.

Ms Parton was either being inspirational or cracking a joke, but the end result is surely the same.

"The sun gets that sinking feeling every night," she said, "but it gets right back up there in the morning."

Thursday — February 21

I MET him at the local swimming pool. He was heading out as I was heading in. In passing chat he told me that "the system" was corrupt, our politicians weren't to be trusted, and there was nothing good in the world. Seeking to change the subject, I asked him where he was off to next.

"Pool reception," he said. "The woman I bought my ticket from gave me a pound too much in my change. I wouldn't want her to have to make it up at the end of her shift."

Nothing good in the world, eh?

People must have wondered why I swam those laps of the pool with such a foolish grin on my face.

Friday — February 22

THINK of manholes and you probably imagine circular iron lids in the middle of the road. You might picture them dirty or rusty. And why should they be anything other than utilitarian? After all, they often cover the entrances to sewers.

But in Japan, manhole covers are sometimes works of art. Some are enamelled, others have abstract designs, some have local emblems on them. It started when local authorities wanted to encourage people to be proud of their new sewage systems – and the fashion caught on.

Lids to sewers! Works of art! Which makes me wonder if there is anything that cannot be beautified, if only we put our minds to it.

Saturday — February 23

THE Scottish writer Robert Louis Stevenson, author of "Kidnapped" and "The Strange Case Of Dr Jekyll And Mr Hyde", was a traveller for the sake of his health, but he was a traveller nonetheless.

He lived north and south in the UK, in France, Colorado, New York State and, finally, on islands in the southern Pacific Ocean. He knew about travelling. He knew the worst and the best of it.

"We are all travellers in the wilderness of this world," he wrote, "and the best we can find in our travels is an honest friend."

Sunday — February 24

THE storyteller Hans Christian Andersen wrote, "Every man's life is a fairy-tale, written by God's fingers."

In many of his stories an innocent finds themselves in a turbulent world. They fear they might sink. Then they have a change of heart, or realise they need God, and things get better. How much does that sound like life?

How much might we – in humility – learn from those tales about finding our own happy ever after?

Monday — February 25

A FRIENDLY word when someone's down,
A comfort when there's doubt,
A helping hand along the way,
And that's what love's about.
A little laughter in life's storms
With time to share a smile,
To show someone the road ahead
Grows smoother with each mile.
To offer hope when times are hard
And watch the sun come out,
To show the world you really care,
And that's what love's about!

– Iris Hesselden.

Taking the high road.

Loch Lomond, Scotland.

Tuesday — February 26

I **HAVE** seen some beautifully intricate patterns woven into the thatched roofs of cottages. But those thatchers had natural straw for their raw material. Could anything as beautiful be done with discarded plastic drinking straws?

A women's co-operative in Uganda, tired of living in poverty and frustrated by a litter problem, began collecting drinking straws. They cleaned them, flattened them, and wove them into mats and coasters. They sold! Eventually, the women began exporting them.

Are they as beautiful as the designs on those thatched roofs? Perhaps not. But do you know what is? The spirit that can make something out of nothing; that can take an impossible situation, wherever it might be, and turn it into a livelihood for friends and family.

Wednesday — February 27

T **HE** great Chinese philosopher Confucius said, "Everything has its beauty – but not everyone sees it." So, if there are things we can't see the beauty in, what should we do? Well, we can settle for what we see at first, or we can spend our lives learning to see more. Perhaps that way we will, eventually, see the beauty in everything. And if we don't? We shall still have seen more by trying.

That Confucius, he's not famous for his foolishness, you know.

Thursday — February 28

R **ONNIE** had helped organise a charity lunch. He wanted to announce how much they had raised. He picked a hand-bell from a shelf. The handle was deeply scored, the clapper had a lump missing, and there was a circular crack running around the rim. But when he swung it the bell made a lovely sound and got everyone's attention.

"Just goes to show," his wife commented. "You don't have to look good and still be in proper working order to serve a useful function."

Ronnie agreed, but he told me later he's not sure if she was talking about the bell, or him!

March

Friday — March 1

IF you wanted to make the world – or at least your part of it – a better place, you could do a lot worse than heed the last words of St David (or Dewi Sant), the Bishop of Mynyw and the patron saint of Wales, who is traditionally celebrated on this day.

His final instruction to his many followers was something each of them could carry out. It was to be faithful in the little things. The little things, like keeping your word, offering a helping hand, being an encourager, putting others first, and so on, require no great plans or preparation. There is no great need to study or practise, and you never need to wait until a more suitable time. You simply live openly, honestly and with compassion, whenever the opportunity presents itself.

Many a saint has built his, or her, reputation on little things done well. You and I might build a good life in exactly the same way.

Saturday — March 2

WANT to control your world?
Yes, but . . .

You can't control the weather. You can't control most of the stuff your body does or doesn't do. How your partner, children or the people you meet will be.

In fact, you can't control a whole lot of stuff that impacts on your life. But you can control your thoughts, your responses to the things that affect you, and the decisions you make because of them. Maybe not easily at first, but increasingly with practice. And, by controlling your decisions, you gradually begin to control your world.

You don't think that will work? Well, then, you're right. It won't work.

See? You made a decision and it became a reality.

Now imagine you had decided differently . . .

Sunday — March 3

THE clacking jackdaws homeward go
As eventide cedes day to night,
The golden orb slides down below
The western sky in glorious light.
Impending darkness in the east
Pursues the pink-splashed blue before,
Serene the scene, a natural feast.
A time to muse there must be more
Than all we see and hear and feel
In God's creation, mystery.
This heavenly sphere, immortal wheel,
Our mother earth, eternity.

– George Hughes.

Monday — March 4

THE wool-coats in these verses by Christina Rossetti refer to the fuzz that often covers buds. The glue-coats will be what hold baby leaves layered over each other until it is time for them to separate and open.

But the phrase that most grabs my attention is "yet a lapse of weeks." In other words, at this bleak time of the year, we need but hold on a few more weeks to see nature work its miracles.

Every valley drinks,
Every dell and hollow;
Where the kind rain sinks and sinks,
Green of spring will follow.

Yet a lapse of weeks
Buds will burst their edges,
Strip their wool-coats, glue-coats, streaks,
In the woods and hedges.

But for fattening rain
We should have no flowers,
Never a bud or leaf again
But for soaking showers.

Tuesday — March 5

ROBERT LOUIS STEVENSON thought that one of the worst things a person could do was develop a facial expression that hid their emotions.

People usually do it as a defence, because they have been hurt, but all too often it becomes a trap.

Stevenson compared those faces to the windows of the houses we live in. We might keep the curtains drawn, or pretend all is well by creating beautiful stained-glass façades.

Good people look on both and have no idea we are inside, longing to be loved.

How much better to keep our "windows" clear, to keep our expressions honest, looking out for those who might hurt, while not shutting out those who want to love?

Open those windows, hang out of them for a while, and greet your fellow man or woman.

Wednesday — March 6

WRITING as an older man, G.K. Chesterton recalled being four years old and going into the garden. Day after day he had an unexplained, but powerful, belief that some treasure was waiting for him.

Whether the treasure was in the ground, in the greenery, or in the air, he did not know, but he never doubted it was there.

The treasure never materialised – or perhaps it did. Looking back, Chesterton was convinced the treasure was the world itself.

Thursday — March 7

THE poet Coleridge once wrote, "Friendship is a sheltering tree." It occurred to me that friendships, just like trees, must have strong roots, they may change with the seasons, they may take a buffeting in rough weather, or be a delight in sunnier times.

But, if you are going to have a tree or a friendship, first of all, someone must plant a seed!

Friday — March 8

THERE is a stairway in a street in Liège that rises for over 400 steps at what must be a 45 degrees angle. That's quite a slog, and I wouldn't like to climb it every day carrying groceries.

You might imagine the locals dislike it, but actually, they use it as a canvas, "painting" giant figures on it in flowers, or illuminating it with candles. And so, something that might have been a major nuisance becomes a tourist attraction for the Belgian town.

The difficulties in our lives tend to hang around, getting in the way – until we apply a little imagination, and put them to a better use!

Saturday — March 9

PEOPLE have gone on quests, climbed mountains to consult gurus, all in search of wisdom. But wisdom might have suggested they simply stay at home.

The 13th-century monk Meister Eckhart wrote that, "Wisdom consists of doing the next thing you have to do, doing it with your whole heart, and finding delight in doing it."

The "next thing" will always have to be done. We get to choose how we do it, and how we do it determines the impact it has on our day.

The wise way is always the way that makes the day a more delightful experience.

Sunday — March 10

IF you can't say something nice . . ."

The old saying has been expressed in many ways across the centuries. But my favourite version comes from the Welsh poet and hymnist Anna Laetitia Waring.

Some time in the 1800s, she wrote:

"If aught good thou canst not say, or thy brother, foe, or friend,
Take thou, then, the silent way, lest in word thou shouldst offend."

Monday — March 11

THE woman's clothes spoke of a difficult life; her accent spoke of a home far away. She showed a toy pram and a baby dolly to the charity shop assistant. They were both "pre-loved" and didn't cost much at all.

But they obviously cost too much. In a language I did not understand, she explained to her three-year-old daughter and put the pram back where it came from.

As she moved towards the counter to pay for the dolly, her daughter held out the coins a departing stranger had put in her hand. Enough for dolly – and her pram, too.

"You can't help every displaced child in the world, you know," I advised the Lady of the House outside the shop.

Then, seeing the moist sheen on her eye, and the firm set of her mouth, I added, "Well, maybe just every one we meet."

Tuesday — March 12

THE spirit soars with sheer delight
To look around and see
Whole rivers of the deepest blue
That ripple round each tree,
And spread like blue lakes through the glades
To glow in dappled light
Like sapphire jewels from the earth,
A truly wondrous sight!

Each breath is fragrant with their scent
So delicate and sweet;
I walk the root strewn path with care
With flowers at my feet.
How difficult it is to go
And leave this scene behind;
Like Wordsworth with his daffodils
I'll see them in my mind!

– Eileen Hay.

Wednesday — March 13

THE end of the barbed wire had once been wrapped around the fence-post, but a foot or so of it had come loose. Walking the path that ran alongside the fence, I had developed a habitual swerve at that point so I didn't catch my clothes on the barbs.

Really, I should have taken a hammer and a staple along with me on one of those walks and fixed that bit of wire back to the post. But, the other morning, tiny sparkling dew-drops showed me an enterprising spider had anchored a beautifully complex web to that ugly curl of wire.

Opportunities to make something better surround us all the time. This time Mr Spider beat me to it!

Thursday — March 14

A MUM asked her young son what he had done at school that day. He thought about it and said, "Well, we played . . ."

"Anything else?" she asked.

"There was some other stuff that was quite important," he told her thoughtfully, "but I can't remember what it was."

Play is not only important to schoolchildren. In whatever form our play takes these days, we should give it all due respect. After all, what would life be without it? Never forget to play!

Friday — March 15

DANNI lives in "a home for adult waifs and strays". The other residents have a variety of unhappy social or psychological problems. She helps out wherever she can, but it's not an environment where appreciation is easily shown.

Recently a resident lost her key. She asked Danni's help and, together, they found it.

Later Danni overheard her telling another resident, "I asked her because everyone knows she cares for us."

"It didn't put another penny in my already penniless purse," Danni told me, "but those few words made me feel like the richest woman in the world."

Beauty in tiny places.

Saturday — March 16

THE writer J.R. Caldwell was on a walking tour of the Scottish Highlands, some time back. He was struck by the apparent poverty of the people who lived there.

As he passed one home, a woman stepped out from the dark interior, shaded her eyes, and basked for a moment in the warmth of the sun.

She didn't notice him, but he was close enough to hear her murmur, "Oh, the whole sun . . . all to myself."

Of course, the sun also shone on Caldwell, and the trees, and the chickens in their run – and for half the world. But, to her, it felt as if the sun shone only for her.

He may have thought her poor, but she didn't.

Likewise, the love of God is for all Creation, but it is also all for you.

And none are poor who can claim that for themselves.

Sunday — March 17

*S*UNDAY *morning stillness settles,*
Silent gulls go flying by;
Sultry clouds are drifting slowly,
Hiding sunbeams in the sky.
Finches, sparrows and a robin
Chase and flit searching for food;
Greedy starlings, cheeky manner,
Changing now the peaceful mood.
Camellia cascades now are shedding,
Dropping rosy flowered heads;
Yellow daffs with orange faces
Glow in budding flower-beds.
In the earth new life is stirring,
Calling as the church bell rings,
Reminding us of God's creation,
The beauty, hope and joy of spring.

– Chrissy Greenslade.

Monday — March 18

WRITING of the month of March, the naturalist Richard Jefferies commented, "How happy the trees must be to hear the song of the birds again in their branches. After the silence and leaflessness to have the birds back once more and to feel them busy at the nest building; how glad to give them the moss and the fibres and the crutch of the boughs to build in."

At times when we feel the best of life is gone, or that what we offer is no longer required, rediscovering, or creating anew, a purpose for the days is like spring arriving in one's life again. Like the returning of the birds.

Tuesday — March 19

THE world will tell us we fool ourselves when we look for the best in people. People will think themselves wise for refraining from such foolishness. Their lives will be lessened by it – but they will think themselves wise.

St Augustine might have been addressing them when he wrote, "Dost thou hold wisdom to be anything other than truth, wherein we behold and embrace the supreme good?"

He didn't think so, and neither do I. Let's be wise enough to work for, and live in, and enjoy the good that is in this world.

Wednesday — March 20

THERE is a lot of work goes into running a food bank, and Jean tells me she does none of it. She assured me she takes no part in collecting, doesn't do any lifting and shifting, none of the paperwork is her responsibility, she never makes up food parcels.

But, three times a week, she goes to the local distribution centre with tins of home baking which she shares with the staff and the people coming in looking for help.

Hmm. Adding a little sweetness to a difficult situation – that's far from nothing, Jean. And I'm not just saying that because she plied me with cakes!

Thursday — March 21

THE people of Costa Rica have a greeting almost exclusive to that country, but it has a meaning we might all take to heart. Where we might say "Hiya" or "Have a nice day", they say, *Pura vida.*" It can mean "Hello", "Goodbye", "Safe travels" or "Enjoy your life", but the actual translation of the phrase is "pure life".

It came from a Mexican movie that was popular there in the Fifties, in which a traveller suffered a seemingly endless series of mishaps but was determined, nonetheless, to live a pure life.

The world might still put obstacles in our way. There's nothing we can do about that. But, let's face it, we can't help but "have a nice day" if we are living a *"pura vida"*.

Friday — March 22

EVERYDAY life asks a lot of us – work, commuting, shopping, upkeep of the home, familial responsibilities – and we often think we are doing well if we can lay aside some time for ourselves.

But, supposing we laid aside time for something greater than us; service, appreciation of beauty, exploration of faith. As the American writer Henry David Thoreau said, "Pursue some path, however narrow, in which you can walk with love and reverence."

That extra discipline will provide a lift to every other aspect of your busy schedule. Find yourself such a path, and never let life become so busy you can't spend some time wandering along it.

Saturday — March 23

THE invisible angel at the pools of Bethesda used to "trouble" the waters to let people know that a time of healing was at hand. The poet John Greenleaf Whittier borrowed the legend to use in a poem about the fierce winds of March.

"Blow, then, wild wind!" he wrote. "Thy roar shall end in singing, The chill in blossoming; Come, like Bethesda's troubling angel, bringing the healing of the spring."

I, for one, am looking forward to the singing!

Tropical paradise.

Costa Rica Beach, Costa Rica.

Sunday — March 24

A FRIEND of mine has a framed enso on his wall. It's a Japanese art form, but at first glance it simply looks like a roughly drawn circle. Actually, it *is* a roughly drawn circle. Sometimes it is done in one stroke of the brush, sometimes it is composed of several strokes.

One of the ideas behind it is that parts of it will be perfect, parts of it will be imperfect, and by encompassing both it becomes a symbol of completion.

Whether that works as art or not is up to the individual viewer, but I like to think it is a good metaphor for life, with the perfect and the imperfect both being needed to complete the picture.

Monday — March 25

THE dance school teacher had stressed the importance of good manners when they went bag-packing. Her pupils were doing well. But as one girl offered to help, the lady snapped at her, saying, "No! I'm particular about how my shopping is packed."

The teacher was about to intervene when the lady put a sizeable donation in the collecting bucket, adding, "But I did so enjoy watching you practise your dance moves in between customers."

Sometimes it's not how you think you ought to behave that makes the difference, but what you do when you think no-one is looking.

Tuesday — March 26

I AM assured by great thinkers that the world and everything in it is beautiful, if we look closely enough to understand its essential nature. I try. I really do. And I am better at it than I once was.

But I sympathise more with Friedrich Nietzsche on the matter, perhaps because he seemed to acknowledge the difficulty of the task, and perhaps because his philosophy allows me to do more than look.

"I want more and more," he wrote, "to perceive the necessary character in things as the beautiful; I shall thus be one of those who beautify things."

Look for beauty everywhere. In the places you don't see it, create it.

Wednesday — March 27

RATHER embarrassingly, I recently found myself arguing with a three-year-old over the lyrics to the theme song for the cartoon "Rastamouse". I said the line went, "Always dere to make a bad ting good." She said it was, "Always there to make a paddling pool."

She insisted my version made no sense, and that at least hers had a paddling pool.

The philosophy behind the actual lyrics doesn't make sense according to the normal expectations of the world. While other TV and movie "good guys" are shooting people and blowing things up, the little Jamaican mouse tries to understand why the bad thing was done and usually brings about a positive outcome for everyone. He is much more in tune with a philosophy of forgiveness and redemption than many of our other fictional heroes are.

Which is all very well and good, but as my little friend pointed out, a paddling pool is always a good thing. I could not argue with that!

Thursday — March 28

I HADN'T heard the term "light-warrior" until recently. I like it! I imagine the best time to be a light-warrior is when your own world seems dark. When you aren't seeing it from anyone else, that's when you need to be the light.

Make it fun! Imagine yourself as an agent in occupied territory, a member of the resistance, but instead of blowing up bridges or Death Stars, lift up someone who would have sunk otherwise, smile at a child, respond to ignorance with kindness.

Those things might not sound like much, but they are actually powerful in a way most of us don't understand because we often don't get to see the end results. A candle doesn't begrudge its light to anyone, or insist they put it to good use. It just shines. And makes its own world brighter at the same time.

As someone once said, "All the darkness in the world cannot extinguish the light of a single candle."

If the world seems like a dark place, we only really have two options.

We can hide in the shadows, or we can shine. Be a light-warrior!

A quiet harbour.

Stromness Church, Orkney.

Friday — March 29

IN the early 1800s there lived, in Stromness in Orkney, an elderly widow who sold the wind! For a modest fee, she would guarantee the captains of sailing vessels a favourable breeze, always with the proviso that they might have to wait a while for it.

At first, I was astounded by her cheek and ingenuity. Then I wondered about those captains. Those were not foolish men. How much, I wondered, did they believe in her powers, and how much were they simply helping out one of their own?

Perhaps it was a bit of both. Looking out for your neighbours can have all sorts of favourable outcomes, after all. And it never hurts to hedge your bets.

Saturday — March 30

I AM sure we all know the expression, "He wouldn't harm a fly." It may have been inspired by John Wesley, one of the founders of the Methodist movement.

A friend once watched a fly land on the back of the great man's hand. He gently brushed it away, saying, "Go, sir. There is room enough for both of us."

The world is a busier place now than it was in Wesley's time, but it is not yet so crowded that we might not extend the very same courtesy to all those we may disagree with.

Sunday — March 31

KATIE posted a selfie online. A friend noticed some blemishes on her complexion and airbrushed them out, thinking he was doing a good thing, and sent her the new and "improved" version.

A better thing to do, of course, is to accept people – especially friends – blemishes and all.

The Apostle Paul's "blemishes" were many, but one in particular he referred to as a thorn in his side. God did not take it away or airbrush it out, and it encouraged Paul always to strive for better. God loved Paul, and his imperfections.

April

Monday — April 1

IT seems to me that we are all – even the most cynical of us – involved in love. We are either happily in it, actively seeking it, remembering it, replacing it with inferior things, or trying (too hard) to show the world we don't need it.

It is the power which, either by its presence or its absence, makes the most difference to the everyday life of humankind. More than that, it even transcends this world.

And yet, much as we talk and sing about it, we understand so little about it.

Almost four hundred years ago Thomas Traherne wrote, "Love is the true means by which the world is enjoyed. Our love to others, and others' love to us. We ought therefore, above all things, to get acquainted with the nature of love.

"For love is the root and foundation of nature; love is the soul of life and crown of rewards."

Can I suggest we get studying?

Tuesday — April 2

THERE is a famously captivating photo, taken by Henri Cartier-Bresson in 1933. It shows a street in Seville, but the picture is taken through a hole in a wall, the street is strewn with rubble, and there appear to be bullet holes in the other walls.

A group of children are at play in the rubble. One is catching a friend, another is holding his sides because he is laughing so much, and a boy on crutches is grinning as he leaves the game behind.

Even in times of war and destruction, children still play. As adults, we might not be able to avoid turbulent times, but we can choose how we respond to them: how we live amidst them.

With a smile and in the company of friends is generally the best way.

Wednesday — April 3

TWO men decided to conduct an experiment. One introduced himself to a homeless man and gave him a hundred dollars. The other secretly filmed the encounter.

When the grateful man gathered his belongings and headed down the street, they followed him. They weren't too surprised to see him go into a store that sold alcohol.

When he came out, they kept following. That's when the surprise came. He went to places where other homeless people congregated. He took the food he had bought out of his bag and gave it away. They were amazed. He, when they told him what they were doing, was surprised that they thought he would do anything else.

They gave him another hundred dollars by way of apology. It seems a cheap price to pay for the lesson that human dignity does not depend on having a permanent home.

Thursday — April 4

IN the 1930s, or thereabouts, the (often whimsical) Irish writer Robert Wilson Lynd considered the ways in which men differed from birds. The greatest difference, he decided, was "in the ways birds build their homes, and yet leave the landscape as it was before."

Not that I'm suggesting we all live in nests, but you get the point.

Friday — April 5

WE have sparks of inspiration always deep inside,
Keep them all shining bright and they will be your guide.
Sometimes we need encouragement to do or say what's right,
To reach out to the ones we know and offer love and light.
But trust that still small voice within and you will do what's best,
A little inspiration will always do the rest.
So if you're undecided just brush away the doubt,
A moment's pause, then once more just let that spark shine out!

– Iris Hesselden.

Saturday — April 6

J.B. PRIESTLEY thought himself a bit of a grumbler. In the late 1940s, according to his son Tom, there was one topic on which he grumbled extensively, and really thought the government of the day ought to do something about. The country had recently been through an epic war and was still struggling to recover. The government was prioritising food and transport, but Priestley felt it ought to put more emphasis on . . . fun!

Not the most practical idea? Perhaps. But we might have been surprised by the results.

I would like to say I never grumble, but I can already imagine the Lady of the House's delicately raised eyebrow.

Perhaps the best any of us can do, if we must grumble, is to do it for such a good cause.

Sunday — April 7

A POET or philosopher, of whom I know nothing else, once wrote, "Give to the world the best that you have, and the best will come back to you."

It may be true, it may not, but consider . . .

If someone else benefits from your best, then that is a good thing. If they benefit and then you also benefit, then that is twice as good!

But, if no-one benefits, if our best is never given out, then we need to ask, "What else am I keeping it for?"

Monday — April 8

APRIL. The month has long been known for its April showers. The Latin word the name comes from is "aperio" and it doesn't mean "showers" – but there is still a connection!

The rain from all of those showers encourages new growth, and flowers and buds begin to open. "Aperio" means "opening."

As we enjoy the arrival of spring and all the beauty that opens up around us, may we contribute to the wonder of it all by opening up our hearts to each other.

Tuesday — April 9

HAD a serious conversation with someone who wondered if it was "less bad" to steal food from supermarkets if that food was nearing its expiry date and had already been reduced in price. It was a very real question for her. Then I watched her walk away with several bags of groceries.

Moments like that just break my heart. But the people who donated the food to the food bank that helped this woman feed her children in a more honest way . . . well, they just heal my heart right back up again!

Wednesday — April 10

HOW good are you at DIY? I have a mixed record with do-it-yourself. Shelves that looked straight when I put them up turned out to lean this way or that – or fell down when the first book was placed on them.

On the other hand, most of the paint I have applied to our walls has stayed on the wall.

Why am I asking this?

Because I don't know how worried I should be by this notion the playwright George Bernard Shaw came up with: "Life isn't about finding yourself," he wrote. "Life is about creating yourself!"

Thursday — April 11

WHEN I see Jack and Davie about town they will, generally, be travelling together. You see, Jack can't see, but he can walk. Davie can't walk, but he can see. So, Jack pushes the wheelchair, trusting Davie's guidance, and Davie keeps up a running commentary on everything he sees. In effect, he is Jack's eyes, and Jack is his feet.

I thought of those fine gentlemen when I heard the Swedish proverb, "When a blind man carries a lame man, both go forward."

We all have shortcomings. What we need is someone who makes up for them. And, for the relationship to be perfect, they should let us to do the same for them in return.

Friday — April 12

THERE is an old story of two men who walked from Leeds to London in search of work. It was an arduous trek. When they arrived in Barnet they were exhausted, but still had ten miles to go to reach their destination.

One man declared it was too much for him. He was giving up. The other man should go on alone.

"Nay, nay!" his friend replied. "We'll gang on together, thee and me. After all, ten miles is nobbut five miles each!"

Journeys always seem half as long when made with a friend, especially when travelling in a common cause.

Saturday — April 13

I LIKE to think I am rarely angry. Then again, if that were true, the Lady of the House could have no reason for presenting me with this verse from Charles and Mary Lamb's children's book "Tales From Shakespeare".

"Anger in its time and place may assume a kind of grace,

It must have some reason in it – and not last beyond a minute!"

If I can't promise never to be angry, I can at least aspire to keeping it within a minute.

Sunday — April 14

THOMAS of Celano wrote three biographies of the founder of his monastic order, Francis of Assisi. But his enthusiasm for the saint was nothing compared to Francis's passion for the natural world.

"The nimble activity and wondrous science of bees," Thomas wrote, "could move him to glorifying the wonders of the Lord so enthusiastically that he would speak of nothing else for the whole day."

A patch of flowers might arouse similar passion. In what surprising places might we find God today?

Monday — April 15

I **COULD** see his reflection in the train window. His seat was in front of mine. His nose was against the glass. He was enthralled by the view – while I read my newspaper!

Something fell down the side of the seat, hitting my shoe.

"My penny!" He couldn't have been more than three years old.

I picked the coin up.

"Is this your penny?" I asked. "Look what it turned into!"

His expression of amazement as he accepted the shiny pound coin (with the nodding approval of Grandad) suited my reasoning. His delight at the scenery I'd been neglecting had reminded me of the importance of appreciation. It can multiply the value of anything, even turning something as base as a disc of copper into a coin of gold.

Tuesday — April 16

T **HERE** is a picturesque castle in Biertan, Romania, with a room that caught my interest. It's called "the Marital Prison." Traditionally, couples considering divorce were expected to live together in the room for six weeks, trying to fix what had gone wrong with their relationship. It seems to have worked. There has been one divorce there in 300 years.

Some might say the reasons for the success of the Marriage Prison are more practical than romantic. For instance, that's six weeks without earning a living.

But, I was struck by the fact that, while in the room, the couple have to share everything. They are given one pillow, one set of cutlery, and so on. Selfishness just would not work in that place, and those who tried to make it work probably shouldn't be married in the first place.

An ideal solution to many forms of conflict is to put the other person's needs first, and know that they, in turn, will do the same for you.

Thankfully, most of us don't have to be locked up to realise that!

The mystical East.

Zhao Xing, China.

Wednesday — April 17

A STUDENT went in search of China's greatest healer. The man he found insisted he wasn't the greatest – only the most famous.

"There is a greater healer," he said. "He cures illnesses as soon as they appear, before they get serious. And there is one greater than him who treats the people and the village in such a way that the illnesses never appear. Because their work is not so dramatic, no-one has heard of them. Because I am not so great, I became skilled at dealing with the most dreadful cases – so my fame spread."

If we want to be famous, when a conflict arises we will win the conflict. If we want to be great, we can nip that conflict in the bud or, greater yet, make sure it never arises in the first place.

Thursday — April 18

S OME, gently, mock the relationship between the very young and the very old. Some, of in-between age, think they would be likewise, if only they weren't so busy making a living.

That may be true, but there may be something else at work.

John Ruskin, a social commentator in the Victorian era, wrote, "Childhood often holds a truth with its feeble fingers, which the grasp of manhood cannot retain, which it is the pride of utmost age to recover."

What is that truth? Ah, if only I were old enough, or young enough, to know!

Friday — April 19

I T was a regular saying of a friend of mine. He was of Yorkshire farming stock, and I transcribe his words here the best I can.

Once a difficult period was over, or a tough job had been completed, he might say, "Why, noo, this 'ere mud hev bin better, but it cud hev bin warse."

On the one hand, it's a way of counting blessings, on the other it's a way of not being too conceited but also avoiding false humility.

My understanding might not be perfect, but it could be worse!

Saturday — April 20

WE all need peace and quiet, Lord,
To help us on our way.
We need to find serenity
To calm a troubled day.
We all need help and comfort,
A beacon in the night,
The gift of love and friendship,
An ever-guiding light.
So thank you, Lord, for being there
Whatever comes our way,
For all the love which never dies,
And thank you for today.

– Iris Hesselden.

Sunday — April 21

THE Philippines are seven time zones ahead of us. As we in the UK are, hopefully, still asleep, Christians over there will be heading to church before sunrise to celebrate Easter.

Grace, a native of those islands now making her home here, tells me her home church begins the service in the dark, in silence, as if in a tomb. Then the pastor leads them out into the light, in the name of the risen Lord.

How beautifully appropriate! May Easter be a journey from darkness into the light for all the countries of the world. He is risen – in every time zone!

Monday — April 22

A NEWSPAPER columnist of the early 20th century used to sign his column *Y.Y.*

Despite the often serious issues he tackled, he always strove to bring a smile to his readers' faces, hence the *nom de plume* at the end.

So, why did he call himself Y.Y.? Because he wanted people to think he was Ys (wise) – and laugh at the very idea!

Tuesday — April 23

WE are never satisfied." How often have you heard it said? Those of us with roofs over our heads rarely think how much we would appreciate them if we were homeless. We might leave a tap running, oblivious to how precious that wasted water might be to another. We complain about the cost of petrol without being thankful we don't have to walk the miles we drive.

We take what we have for granted, focusing our desires on having more. But there is never enough for those who go that way. What might work is if we turned our attention in the other direction, appreciating anew everything we already have.

What might we find? Well, the essayist Leigh Hunt wrote, "The commonest objects are only wonders at which habit has made us cease to wonder."

Which would you choose? Striving ever onwards, never being satisfied, or rediscovering our sense of wonder and the miracles that fill even the commonest life?

Wednesday — April 24

KATHERINE BUTLER HATHAWAY was born in 1890 and suffered from a spinal condition which saw her strapped to boards for extended periods to bring about a cure. The treatment failed. She required constant care through a childhood which she nevertheless described as happy.

Later in life, she decided to buy her own home and set it up as a creative space, but this meant moving away from her family and nursing care. It was a very scary decision.

She described it like this:

"There and then I invented this rule for myself, to be applied to every decision I might have to make in the future. I would sort out all the arguments and see which ones belonged to fear and which to creativeness, and other things being equal I would make the decision which had the largest number of creative reasons on its side.

"I think it must be a rule something like this that makes jonquils and crocuses come pushing through the cold mud."

Thursday — April 25

GETTING on to the ridge is the difficult part. Once you are on it there is a path, worn by generations of boots, that rises and falls over the connected peaks.

This was where I found the wise man. He was soaking up the sunshine. I looked to the other side of the path, where the ground fell into a deep corrie, shaded from the sunshine and still under a blanket of snow.

"Isn't it a little early for that sort of thing?" I asked.

"Depends which side of the hill you choose to lie on."

I noticed the rucksack, the camping stove, the walking poles, the half-eaten chocolate bar. Not the typical image of a mountaintop guru, but a wise man nonetheless.

Friday — April 26

ARE there habits in your life you feel you might be better without? Things you do that you wish you didn't do? People will tell you to resist your temptations, to fight them, do all you can to prevent them having a say in your life.

And I couldn't disagree with any of that. Except, the more we focus on our problems, the bigger they seem to become. It's almost like we empower them by paying attention to them.

Of course, we shouldn't ignore them totally, but we might change focus. Imagine we gave the same attention to and invested the same energy in those positive things we would have replace our negative attributes. We might find the former gradually edges the latter out.

Saturday — April 27

THE great evangelist and preacher Billy Graham was talking about marriage when he said, "We need to learn to say, 'I was wrong; I'm sorry.' And we also need to reply, 'That's all right; I love you'."

It occurred to me that after we had learned to do those things in our closest relationships, we might also begin to spread them further afield.

Sunday — April 28

SPURGEON'S is a theological college in Croydon. Its crest is a hand holding a cross, and the Latin motto "Et Teneo, Et Teneor," meaning "I hold, and I am held." Holding tight to the cross, the students are being held in the hands of God.

It's a philosophy that might be taken beyond the walls of the college. Imagine if we held our neighbour's wellbeing, gently and carefully, in our hands, just as ours is held in His.

Monday — April 29

THE ancient well would have been ornate enough in its original state. Situated in the garden of a stately home, it had carved lion heads at the four quarters. Peacocks provided the base carvings and hunting birds topped the design off. Between these a leafy design filled the spaces.

But recently someone had filled in the spaces between the leaves with little pieces of broken glass held in place by clear resin. Now, in almost every light and from almost any angle, the well has a magical sparkle about it.

I am informed the glass came from bottles broken in and around the gardens. Such simple things show us that redemption and renewal are truly possible. Beauty from broken things? Well, well!

Tuesday — April 30

POETS and philosophers like to talk of roads and paths. We have the road not taken, the path through the woods, the road less travelled, walk where there is no path and create your own, and so on. But the Austrian poet Franz Werfel, who lived and worked between and during the World Wars, suggested there might be a better route.

"Which road did you take," the poet asked, "that brought you here at last?"

"No road," was the reply. "No road did I take. I leaped. I leaped from dream to dream."

May

Wednesday — May 1

IT shines just like a candle
That flickers in the breeze,
So that, in the darkest night,
The truth one always sees.
So forget not the ingredient
That helps us all to cope,
That magical elixir is, of course,
Quite simply, Hope.

– Brian H. Gent.

Thursday — May 2

IMAGINE if someone invented a way to make artificial gold that was indistinguishable from the natural kind. The price of gold would drop like a stone. It would no longer be a precious metal.

In the early 19th century production of aluminium was prohibitively expensive. So rare and "precious" was the finished product that, in 1860, Emperor Napoleon III had a few pieces of cutlery made out of it. The less important guests at his banquets had to make do with gold and silver cutlery. His favoured few dined with aluminium knives and forks.

What would those illustrious guests make of the fact that, these days, people drink out of aluminium cans, or that we use aluminium foil for baking, and then we throw it away? It is so commonplace it is disposable.

What is the point I am making? I suppose it is that we should be careful what we believe is valuable in this life, and think twice about what we regard as treasure.

Friendship, love, kindness, family . . . those are as precious now as they ever have been. And I can't see them losing their value any time soon.

Friday — May 3

JACK was taking an evening stroll along the beach. He noticed some young folk had started a campfire. There was music, laughter, alcohol, and various rowdy shenanigans. As the sun started to set the group grew more sedate.

While the sky went through a parade of dazzling colours most of them stood up to watch. And when the last flash of the sun disappeared beyond the ocean, several of them gave it a round of applause.

"I could understand them watching it," he said to me, "but applause?"

I guess we like to appreciate, but more than that, there is something in us that likes to say, "Thank you", whether we know who we are thanking or not.

Saturday — May 4

A WISE person said, "If you knew all, you would forgive all." The point is that no-one chooses to be bad and if you knew the events that shaped them in such an awful way your heart would fill with pity.

I would add, if you understand those words and believe them to be true, then you don't even need to know all. Knowing that you would forgive, you might as well just go ahead and forgive.

Sunday — May 5

PLATO once asked, "What evil might people do if no-one could see them doing it?"

I prefer Jesus's idea that we should do our good deeds in secret. When we feed the hungry, we shouldn't go showing off about it.

If people could do what they liked in secret and get away with it, would they do evil or good? Both, I imagine, as they do now. But, as it does now, good would overwhelm the other stuff. That's no secret!

Time for you.

Monday — May 6

IT'S an old Buddhist saying, but it's new to me. And, like all the great philosophies, such as "Love one another" and "Do unto others as you would have them do unto you", it is remarkably simple.

"As a bee gathering nectar does not harm or disturb the colour and the fragrance of the flower; so do the wise move through the world."

The Hollywood star and eco-warrior Woody Harrelson described his personal lifestyle in a similar fashion when he said, "I want to leave a light footprint in this world."

And, in truth, the wiser we are and the softer we are with this beautiful world the longer it will remain a beautiful world.

Tuesday — May 7

DID you ever envy someone in a position of fame or power? It's an all-too-human instinct. And yet, those people might often envy things we have.

When eighteen-year-old Alexandrina Victoria became Queen Victoria she also became one of the most powerful and wealthy women the world has ever known. And yet, she was often lonely. One of her closest companions was Dash, the pet spaniel who had loved her before she was Queen. On a memorial erected for Dash, Victoria had written, "His attachment was without selfishness, his playfulness without malice, his fidelity without deceit."

If you have a friend like that, reader, you need envy no-one, ever.

Wednesday — May 8

IN 1799 Royal Marine Major Thomas Oldfield wrote that there was nothing in this world worth doing a mean action for; much less an unjust one. Yet, sometimes, to one degree or another, we still do.

But, when we do, we could do worse than think along the major's lines and ask, what was the reason? Then ask, was it worth it? And, might I act, and live, for better, nobler reasons?

Thursday — May 9

SYDNEY is the niece of an American friend. In her early twenties, she was taking the chance to travel the world. So, while she was in the neighbourhood, the Lady of the House and I took her out to dinner and a visit to the botanical gardens.

While we were there an older man saw her taking photographs of various plants. He asked her thoughts on correct lighting for a particular shot. It soon became obvious he didn't have a camera; he was just lonely and looking for someone to talk to.

Despite having other things to do, and us giving her the opportunity to move on, Sydney stayed, and she talked.

And, of course, we watched from a few shrubs away.

That's when my sweetheart put her arm around mine, nodded at our young friend and said, "Patience and kindness; are there any more beautiful flowers in all the gardens of the world?"

Friday — May 10

*O*UR *lives have many problems*
With lessons we must learn,
And there are things to challenge us
At every twist and turn.
We're told to count our blessings,
It's sometimes hard to do,
And yet the world is wonderful
It's there for me and you.

And though sometimes the sky is dark
The clouds will move away,
A hopeful new awareness
Will lift and light the day.
So greet each new tomorrow
Whatever comes along,
This life has much to offer.
Be cheerful and be strong!

– Iris Hesselden.

Saturday — May 11

THE 13th-century priest Thomas Aquinas once said, "Man cannot live without joy."

Now, I know some people live lives where happiness is scarce, but others who have ample opportunity for joy seem to prefer not to indulge. I was once saddened to hear a friend say, "We aren't here to be happy." He may be right, but surely we might as well be happy while we do whatever it is we are here for.

It is possible to live without joy, but there are many ways to live, and joyfully is surely one of the best.

Sunday — May 12

THE University of Virginia experimented on the difference having a friend nearby made to an individual's pain. People's brains were monitored as painful stimuli were administered. If they were on their own, or holding a stranger's hand, the pain sensors lit up. If they held a friend's hand, the reaction was less intense.

Interesting. But I wish they had also monitored the friends' brains. Despite having no pain administered to them, I am sure they would have felt it all the same.

For better or worse, friends share.

Monday — May 13

THERE'S a joke about a teacher teaching basic arithmetic who asked, "If I gave you two rabbits, Johnny, then I gave you another two, how many rabbits would you have?" Johnny replied, "Six!"

The teacher gave him another chance to get it right, and another. She was about to give up in frustration when another child said, "Please, Miss. Johnny already has two rabbits at home."

It's a reminder that what might seem like a simple truth to us might not be the same to someone else. Their experience might mean they bring something different to the discussion. Let's always be prepared for those extra rabbits.

"Yes, I am cute, aren't I?"

Tuesday — May 14

WILLIAM PENN, who founded the State of Pennsylvania, wrote that we should "have an indifferency for more than what is sufficient. Be rather bountiful than expensive."

Which reminded me of the more recent saying: "If you have more than you need, build a bigger table."

When we have what is sufficient, we are more blessed than many in this world. What should our response be? Thankfulness. And beyond that? Making sure that as many people as possible have the chance to be similarly thankful.

Wednesday — May 15

THE road to the railway station is lined with trees. Some time ago, perhaps to prevent leaves blowing on to the tracks, the trees were pollarded. In other words, they were cut right back to the trunk. If trees had feelings, I imagine they would have been traumatised.

For some reason, the practice was discontinued on the left side several years ago, and only recently stopped on the right side. The trees on the right are beginning to push out little branches now, and new leaves. But the trees on the left are majestic, almost back to their former height. When covered with leaves you would never know they had been so harshly treated.

Sometimes, we might feel "pollarded" by life, cut back, useless. But persevere. Push out those "branches". They will seem small and ineffective at first but, with patience and perseverance, you will stand tall again one day.

Thursday — May 16

GOT a problem? Set the committee to work.
Who are the committee? They are a resource available to most of us. And they don't charge for their good work.

John Steinbeck described them and their work like this: "It is a common experience that a problem difficult at night is resolved in the morning after the committee of sleep has worked on it."

Friday — May 17

MET Harry at a wooden bench atop a high hill. He invited me to sit and the dogs sprawled out in the grass. We sat there in silence for a while, soaking up the waving grass, the darker green of the treetops beneath us, the misty blue shimmer of the sky, the birdsong, and the breeze on our faces.

"You're an intelligent man," he said eventually. "And educated."

I nodded, perhaps a little immodestly. After a few more silent moments, he sighed happily.

"Can you feel it? Do you understand it?"

I knew I felt undeserved peace. I was unexpectedly content. I felt a part of something vast and yet, somehow, separated from it. Valued, insignificant, part, apart, in awe.

"No. I don't understand it at all."

But perhaps the understanding – despite our years of life, our education, and our philosophising – is for another, and our job is simply to sit there and say, "Wow!"

Saturday — May 18

SOME say if you make yourself smile it will make you feel happier. I'm not talking about the fake smiles put on to please others.

The Victorian philosopher William James called this the "as if principle." He thought that people put the cart before the horse when it came to their feelings. They waited until they felt good before they laughed.

He suggested they laugh, and they would feel good. People waited until they felt energetic before they exercised. He suggested they exercise, and they would feel energetic.

Their feelings were an after-effect of their activities or situations. James suggested shaping those activities and situations to generate the feelings they wanted. If they lived "as if" they were happy, they would be happy.

At first, I thought the principle disingenuous, a little fake. But then I was happy. And, happily, I can muster no argument against that.

Sunday — May 19

THE Iguazu Falls are not as well-known as other waterfalls like Victoria or Niagara. Which is strange, because, at one and a half miles long, consisting of hundreds of separate falls, they aren't short of magnificence.

On one of the rock faces, however, is a plaque that puts this marvel of the natural world in perspective. It says, "Mightier than the thunders of many waters, mightier than the waves of the sea, the Lord on high is mighty.

"God is always greater than all of our troubles."

Monday — May 20

ALFRED, LORD TENNYSON, was at a low point in his life when he wrote the "Lyrical Monologue" that includes the lines, "I look at all things as they are, but through a kind of glory."

What a way to look at the world! Both bad and good. Whether there is a real glory there to be seen, or whether by looking at the world we add the glory, is still debated.

But of the end result there is no doubt. Glory!

Tuesday — May 21

DO you ever wish you could live a better life? A finer life? Would you, perhaps, like to live your faith a little more openly and fully? But you don't, because this world isn't very accepting of that sort of thing.

It's a fair enough assessment. But . . .

Mahatma Gandhi suggested, "If we could change ourselves, the tendencies in the world would also change. As a man changes his own nature, so does the attitude of the world change towards him."

If you live in a world hostile to the finer things, that's all the more reason to show it the value, the beauty, of those things. As you change your approach, the world might also change its response. Wouldn't that be fine?

Wouldn't that be beautiful?

The mighty force of nature.

Iguazu Falls, on the border of Brazil and Argentina.

Wednesday — May 22

*L*ET *me see with the eyes of a child,*
The beauty, hope and joy,
Recapturing the wonder, Lord,
The world cannot destroy.
We all grow up and miss so much,
The magic fades to grey,
The happy, bright awareness
Is lost along the way.
Lord, let me look with childish eyes
And marvel every day!

– Iris Hesselden.

Thursday — May 23

SOMEONE, a few streets from Harry, uprooted a clump of daffodil bulbs and left them on the pavement by the bins. Harry's too soft-hearted to leave a living thing on a pavement. So, he took it home, found a space in the garden, and made it feel at home.

Eventually the daffs came up and Harry regretted ever thinking he could have too many. But there was more. Pink and yellow lillies rose up and arched over their humbler brethren.

"I'd no idea they were there," Harry said. "Such a bonus!"

I understood his delight. Something similar, but more wonderful, often happens when we do the same for people. We might not need to plant and water them, but they often flower in the most unexpected ways.

Friday — May 24

THE Compliments Man is a busker with a difference. He walks the streets of his home city with a sign identifying himself. If people approach him, he compliments them. If they feel better afterwards, they leave a donation.

"It's not hard work," he says. "Human beings are basically wonderful, which is a good starting point."

Saturday — May 25

KNOW a man who cuts his grass once a year – if that often. But I have seen him spread a blanket in the middle of his mini-meadow and sleep there on a sunny afternoon.

I know a couple who can spend hours on the details of their borders and raised beds without speaking to each other – but they both see it as a meditation.

I know a grandad who takes great care of his lawn only to have his grandsons trample it to mud with their knock-about football matches. Then, once the summer holidays are over, he sets about repairing it all, content that it has been well used.

I thought of all of these and more when I visited the Chalice Well Gardens near Glastonbury Tor which is "a recognised World Peace Garden, dedicated to providing a refuge for all in this troubled world."

Gardens are a gift of peace to all our souls. If we don't have one we should find one to visit. If we do have one then we ought to appreciate it. We might share it with family and friends or, at the very least, soak up all the peace it has to offer, and share that!

Sunday — May 26

I SHOULD have stayed in bed," I say.
"There's nothing going right today."
I burnt the toast and lost my purse,
And later things got even worse.

I stubbed my toe and knocked my knee,
What else was there in store for me?
But later, as I sipped my tea,
I looked at things quite differently.

Had I not heard the birds' sweet song
When I awoke, to cheer me on?
And as it shone around, I saw
The purse which I'd been looking for!

– Joan Zambelli.

Monday — May 27

THE photograph was of earth long dried in the sun. The ground had cracked and curled. But overnight a slight dew had formed. The moisture was mostly burned away by the rising sun, but some remained, a few inches down, in the shadows.

Also in those shadows were seeds, blown there by the warm breeze. Little shoots rose up, protected from the sun and the wind by the walls of the cracks, and soon the desert floor was covered in little purple and pink flowers.

The situation can look very bleak, but sometimes it is the brokenness, the cracks in our lives, that allows new life, new beginnings, to blossom.

Tuesday — May 28

OFTEN great spiritual concepts can come down to some very practical realities. Like Nelson Mandela's advice on optimism. He wrote that an important part of it was "keeping one's head pointed towards the sun, one's feet moving forward."

Optimism may not come easily, but each of us can walk towards it.

Wednesday — May 29

MARY was sitting by the duck pond in the park. A gentle breeze lifted the hair from her forehead and I realised her eyes were closed. Was she sleeping? Was she ill?

"Mary," I said softly. "What are you doing?"

"I'm a human being, Francis," she said without opening her eyes.

"Well, of course you are," I replied. "I know that."

She opened her eyes and turned that mischievous smile on me.

"You don't understand. Usually, I'm doing something. I have a busy life, and I'm glad of it. But sometimes you need a break, a chance to simply be. So, today, surrounded by the water, the grass, the air and the sunshine, I'm not a human doing. I'm a human . . . being!"

Thursday — May 30

I WAS listening to Bobbi Gibb, the first woman to run the Boston Marathon. Back then, authorities were convinced that women weren't physically capable of such a feat.

She calls the Boston Marathon "a big love-in, with people there of all ages, sexes, nationalities."

For they're all in the same metaphorical boat. They have something immense ahead of them to which they will bring all their unique abilities, disabilities, training and so on.

They will face the challenge *en masse*, but they will have to complete it individually. It is much bigger than their differences.

Life is the challenge we all face. We tackle it in our own personal ways, but we are all running in the same race.

Friday — May 31

THE streets in new housing estates are often named randomly. Some, near us, are named after lochs and mountains. Older streets might be named after battles, far-flung parts of the Empire, soldiers or politicians. Some are named after people who lived there before anyone thought to give every street a name.

Like Godliman Street, near St Paul's Cathedral in London. No-one knows who the man was, but they remembered he lived there.

And when they were looking for a street name, well, it was already known as the Godly Man's street.

Most of the streets we live on these days already have names, but if where you lived was to be named after some characteristic you showed above all others, what would it be called?

These verses from "The Loom Of Time" are written by an anonymous poet:

"Not 'til the loom is silent and the shuttles cease to fly,
Shall God reveal the pattern and reveal the reason why.
The dark threads were as needful in the weaver's skilful hand
As threads of gold and silver for the pattern which He planned."

June

HARRY found me on the bridge over the stream.
"The side of the bridge a man leans on tells me a lot about him," he said. "If you watch the stream coming towards you, it tells me you're the kind of man who likes to receive. If you watch the water flowing away, you're the kind of man who likes to give."

Just then, Frank arrived on his bike. He dismounted and Harry recapped his philosophy.

Frank nodded.

"However, if you stand two abreast on a narrow bridge over the stream, it tells me you are the kind of men who need to get out of the way."

Whatever your philosophy for life, it needs to be practical, and a help.

Never a hindrance.

DEAR Lord, you know I long for
A faith that's strong and sure,
That holds me when I'm anxious,
Or lost or insecure.
A faith which questions daily
Yet hankers not for proof,
A faith which seeks for answers
Yet knows its inner truth.
Dear Lord, I'm still imperfect,
My faith may sometimes fail,
I am not always trusting when fears and doubts assail,
Yet hold me, if you will, Lord, whene'er my faith feels small,
For this I know for certain –
Your love won't let me fall.

– Maggie Ingall.

Monday — June 3

HAVE you ever wondered how a flower feels as it spreads its petals in the sunshine? It's an unusual question, I grant you, but it was a beautiful day and I had nothing else to wonder about.

Franz Werfel, the Austrian poet who, in 1941, wrote "The Song Of Bernadette", may have described it accidentally.

"Happiness is . . . the grace to unfold . . . all the spiritual gifts planted within you."

So – happy. That's how I imagine the flower feels.

Tuesday — June 4

THERE is beauty in every soul! But sometimes the world buries it under distractions and responsibilities.

William Soutar was a Perthshire laddie who served in the Royal Navy during World War I. Returning home at the end of it, he went to university, intent on an education and a career. But he became ill and tests were done.

After discovering a serious illness which would curtail his health and limit his work options, Soutar wrote, "I halted in the dusk beside the pillars of West St George's, Edinburgh, and stood for a moment bareheaded, saying over to myself, 'Now I can be a poet!'"

What would you do – what beauty might you create – if there were no other distractions?

Wednesday — June 5

THERE is a line in the book of Proverbs that says, "He who has a generous eye will be blessed." It goes on to talk about giving bread to the poor – which is one sort of generosity. But I liked the idea of a generous eye.

If we look at this world kindly we see kindness, and if we look at it generously we will forgive its faults before they grow big enough (in our minds) to block the view of all the beauty out there.

Look, always, with a generous eye!

Yorkshire sunset.

Knaresborough, North Yorkshire.

Thursday — June 6

IT'S an unobtrusive little street, probably not known for much, but it is home to many, and children play there. It's called Darg Street.

The area around it was once a mining community, and for the many hard-working miners "the darg" meant the day's work, or the amount of coal they shifted.

No coal is mined there now, but raising families, keeping homes going . . . there's a darg as difficult, as noble and as important as any other!

Friday — June 7

THE little girl came down the slide, squealing with laughter. Her mum and gran were waiting at the bottom to catch her.

"Oh, to be young again," I commented with a wistful smile.

"Oh, I wouldn't have it back," Gran replied. "I gave my youth to my daughter. She passed it on to my granddaughter. Now, I've been able to enjoy it three times over!"

Three times young! I would never have thought of it that way.

Saturday — June 8

PEOPLE behave differently In different parts of the country. Apparently. Regional characteristics are distinct and almost sacrosanct. So they say. For the writer J.B. Priestley, in the West Riding of Yorkshire "fault-finding and blame are constant and hearty." Praise and encouragement were a "soft southern trick."

For myself, I have rarely been closer to Heaven than in the West Riding. The people there I count among the most hospitable I have met.

Things change, of course. The people who began them, who continued them and encouraged them, were just that – people. They had no more or less say in the matter than you or me.

If we don't like how our area is seen elsewhere, then we can change it. The new regional characteristics might easily begin with how we talk to our neighbours or visitors.

Sunday — June 9

THE photograph was of a Chinese woman with a basket on her back. The basket held many long-stemmed flowers, picked from the field and destined for the market.

In front of her a small boy offered a handful of the same flowers. They had not been picked with skill, they would never have sold, but the delight on her face was obvious.

In the same way, we have nothing to offer God that He does not already have plenty of (or that He did not create) but, as the woman in the picture could assuredly testify, the gift is not always the contents of the hands.

Often, it is the love in the heart of the giver.

Monday — June 10

STRAWBERRIES might be picked, ripe, any time from late April through to August. Raspberry season is generally a bit later. Crops are usually harvested from August to October in northern Europe. Different fruits and crops ripen at different times throughout the year across the world.

But Rev. Dr Martin Luther King Jr. reminds us there is one "fruit" that is always in season.

"The time is always ripe," he said, "to do right."

Tuesday — June 11

NOAH PURIFOY was, amongst other things, an "assemblage artist." His first major works were constructed from the debris left behind after a riot. Later works included materials from scrap yards and abandoned train carriages.

It's one thing to find or create beauty in a beautiful life. But not everyone is given such a life.

The world owes a special thank-you to those, like Purifoy, who live in more troubled times, take the brokenness of such times, and reassemble them into something more beautiful.

Wednesday — June 12

THE note was included in a scrapbook of advice passed on to a new bride in the days before indoor plumbing.

WASHING CLOTHES: Build a fire in backyard to heat a kettle of rain-water. Shave one cake of lye soap into boiling water. Sort things. Make one pile for whites, one for coloured, one for work-clothes and rags.

To make starch, stir flour in cool water until smooth, then thin down with boiling water. Take white things, rub dirty spots on the washboard. Scrub hard, then boil. Rub coloured clothes and don't boil, just wrench and starch.

Take things out of the kettle with broom stick, then wrench and starch. Hang old rags on the fence. Spread tea towels on grass. Pour dirty water into flower bed. Scrub the porch with the hot soapy water. Turn tubs upside down.

Go put on a clean dress, smooth your hair with combs. Brew up a cup of tea. Sit and rock a while and count your blessings.

Because life isn't all about chores!

Thursday — June 13

THE medical seminar was pretty dry stuff. But Anne did sit a little straighter when one speaker promised an "intervention" that would make all their processes run smoother, would increase the effectiveness of their treatments, and speed up recovery times.

She got really excited when he told his audience that the intervention was free. What could possibly make such a difference and be free, she wondered.

The speaker assured them that what he was talking about was already in place in every medical facility up and down the land, but many of the staff were just too busy hitting targets and filling in forms to be able to use it. It was kindness.

"I was tempted to be annoyed," Anne said, "but the more I thought about it, the more I realised he was right."

Now, how might we make better use of that miracle-working intervention in our work, our social group and our homes?

Friday — June 14

KATIE loves her house, but not its location. There's a road to one side, a railway on another and a high wall on the third. The only "nature" she can see is some bushes and long grass that grow by the wall, beyond her fence. Not very inspiring. Until the mother fox Katie didn't know was there gave birth to her cubs!

Now Katie gets to watch them play and grow from her bedroom window. What she thought of as walled-off wasteland is now a safe and happy creche for the cubs.

Saturday — June 15

I BUMPED into someone I hadn't spoken with in a while. We asked after each other's families, discussed the weather and, mere minutes later, we recalled a kindness that some anonymous Good Samaritan had done for her.

What's so unusual about that? Well, the kindness had been done twenty-seven years previously!

So, if ever you are tempted to do something nice for someone and you wonder if it will be worth it, just remember that. Twenty-seven years!

Sunday — June 16

DON'T wish me Happy Father's Day," he growled. "I'm a fraud! What I do doesn't compare with all my wife does for our family."

"Have you ever left them?" I asked.

"Of course not!" he replied.

"Have you ever let them down?" I asked.

"I try really hard not to," he replied.

"Then you are right," I declared. "You don't do as much as your wife. But you provide the foundations she builds on and the security your children grow in. And that's not nothing."

Then, I took advantage of him being momentarily lost for words to add, "Happy Father's Day!"

Playtime is over.

Monday — June 17

CHUCK CLOSE is an artist who works with photo-imagery and tapestry. He prefers wall-sized works which take a long time to complete. He once said, "A quilt may take a year to complete, but if you keep doing it you get a quilt."

Quilting has never been a speedy occupation and it was often done as a communal activity, which adds an extra dimension to Mr Close's words. If you just keep going in whatever pursuit, you will get there. If you do it with others, you will get there with friends who have grown dearer, having shared your journey.

Tuesday — June 18

ARISTOTLE wrote that, "Happiness is the meaning and purpose of life, the whole aim and end of human existence."

Really? Just happiness? Not something more serious and profound?

Perhaps. But a happy life is no frivolous, lightweight thing. For the man or woman of conscience to be happy they need to have fulfilled their responsibilities, provided for their families, built a home, and (surely) done whatever they can to make sure their neighbours also live a life free from hurt or need. On top of that, they might feel a call to be a good steward of the natural world around them.

Happiness – meaningful happiness – is no easy thing to attain. One might dedicate a life to it, and feel the time very well spent.

Wednesday — June 19

IRONICALLY, just before I read some advice on decluttering the home, a friend arrived with half a dozen DVDs he had borrowed from me.

The advice? "Pick things up, one at a time. If they spark joy in your heart, keep them. If they don't, bin them."

Did the DVDs cause me joy? Well, he had borrowed them five years previously, and I hadn't missed them. So, I offered them to someone else I thought would get a lot of joy from them.

And I saw the spark!

Thursday — June 20

JUST went for a walk in the rain, and didn't get wet! Actually, Warren did the walking. He has been housebound recently, recovering from an illness. A passionate gardener, he hasn't been able to do much in the garden, but a light shower was bringing out the best in it.

So, dressed in woollies and wellies and armed with his phone, he took a slow walk around it, telling the stories of all his plants and garden ornaments.

As he did so, he broadcast it via social media and I could tell he was being watched in the UK, Japan, Oman and Australia. The list of thanks and comments of appreciation was extensive, despite Warren being completely alone.

Social media has many pluses and minuses. Like most things, it depends on how you use it.

Taking people from around the world on a walk round your garden in the rain, to share what you love, has to be one of the most beautiful uses I have encountered so far.

And it begs the question, how do we share what we love?

Friday — June 21

AMONG other things, Andy is a picture hanger. Recently, he was asked to hang some artworks in preparation for a family moving into a house. One large painting was from the 1800s, worth thousands of pounds. Hanging it was a challenge he relished, getting every detail perfect and appreciating the beauty of the art.

His spirits came down to earth with a bump when he turned to the next job — 50 framed family snapshots to be hung in the hall.

He was sure it would be a grindingly boring chore. But the happiness, the tender touches, the looks of love in those casual pictures soon won him round.

He ended up arranging them as carefully as he had the larger, older piece.

Beauty and inspiration can be found in great works, for sure, but let us never forget to also look for them in the everyday.

Saturday — June 22

IT won't be too obvious at first, but from here on, as we head past the summer solstice, the days get shorter. Some people will hardly notice, but others will be more affected by the decrease in sunlit hours. There isn't much we can do about It. That's just the way the world spins.

But we can be sunshine in each other's lives. And, as we find people in darkening places, may we shine all the brighter for them. In doing so, we also light up our own world.

Sunday — June 23

A LOVELY wedding, the bride in white
All billowing tulle and sheer delight,
She clasps a delicate freesia spray,
A pretty touch upon the day –
A little page, sweet and serene
Shoos a magpie off the green.
The day recorded, the selfies done,
The bride and groom's new life has begun.
Joy and happiness for them we pray
As the bells ring out, on this perfect day.

– Dorothy McGregor.

Monday — June 24

TRAMPS regularly visited the farm where Elizabeth grew up. Perhaps they were unemployed, perhaps they were damaged by war, perhaps it was a chosen lifestyle. But they were always hungry.

Elizabeth would hide in fields, away from the farmhouse, so she could watch the men eat the sandwiches with jam or honey Mamma always gave them.

"I was fascinated," she said. "But too young then to know by what. I learned kindness from Mamma. But, watching from the fields, that's where I learned appreciation!"

Tuesday — June 25

HANNAH WHITALL SMITH, a prominent part of the Holiness Movement in the late 1800s, said, "Our lives are full of supposes. Suppose this should happen, or suppose that should happen; what could we do; how could we bear it?"

Modern therapies suggest that many problems lie in resentments about the past, or fear for the future, but that we ought to focus on how we are right now. Because, 99 times out of 100, how we are right now – in this moment, whenever it may be – is fine!

Wednesday — June 26

THE explorer, TV presenter and youngest-ever Chief of the Scout Association Bear Grylls said, "I've seen extreme bravery from the least likely of people. Life is about the moments when it's all gone wrong. That's when we define ourselves."

The chaotic times in life often come as a surprise.

But, what is no surprise to me, or Mr Grylls, is that the meek and the mild, the people we would least expect to have such heroism in them, are very often the ones who rise to the challenge and put it all to rights.

I have a special place in my heart for "the least likely of people."

Thursday — June 27

MY new neighbour and I don't have much in common. She's female and I'm male. She's single, I'm married. She's into healthy living, I'm . . . not. Several decades separate us in age.

But! I recently discovered that we both, in our very different childhoods, sat in cupboards under the stairs, with the doors open just enough so there was light to read by.

Compared to the one special thing we had in common, none of the differences really seemed to matter.

We could do a lot worse, when meeting new people, than search for that one special thing.

Friday — June 28

THE past is gone, it's left behind,
There is no turning back,
But strong in love, in faith and hope
There's nothing more we lack.

We must keep moving forward now,
No time for standing still,
And see the bright horizon shine
Above the distant hill.

So don't regret the passing time
Forget the stress and strife,
To everything a season . . .
Reach out to love and life!

– Brian H. Gent.

Saturday — June 29

IN 2014, a sink-hole opened under a car museum. The floor and several cars fell into the depths. One was the millionth of a particular make to come off the assembly line. It was highly prized – and extensively damaged. A lot of effort was put into hoisting it out the hole, repairing and replacing parts and finding a new, safer place to display it.

Now, do we know any people who might be "in a hole"?

Sunday — June 30

ONE part of Great-aunt Louisa's garden had a steep slope. She wrote in her diary that "Whatever is planted there, after it breaks the soil, seems to take a few days to decide which direction to grow in." The Lady of the House adapted the next line. "Of course, no matter the incline, the shoots eventually reach for the sun." Or, as my sweetheart explained it, "When the ground seems to shift beneath your feet, reach for the Son."

July

Monday — July 1

BRUCE SPRINGSTEEN talked, on the radio, about his childhood, how they lived in poverty much of the time, how many of those around him had self-destructive or even dangerous mind-sets.

But then there was his mother and her two sisters. Those ladies were relentlessly optimistic, insisting things would work out and demanding that life be beautiful. They sound amazing and I am sure they were blessings in his life.

It's a huge disappointment to some people that life isn't beautiful for them. There's an understanding that we might have a role to play in making that beauty come about. Then, there's the more mature understanding that we are the beauty in our life.

All the potential the world has for kindness, love and appreciation exists in each of us. Will we be like those Springsteen remembered who had negative outlooks, or will we be like his mother and aunts who not only demanded life be beautiful, they made it so?

Tuesday — July 2

KRUMMHOLZ is the German word for "crooked wood" and it describes the trees that grow in exposed places. You often see them, stunted and misshapen, on coastal cliff-tops where they are bombarded by salt-water rain and Atlantic gusts. They grow on the high hills where the soil may only be inches thick and icy winds scour the peaks.

But they grow where little else does, they raise their heads above the parapets, they take a chance on life and, despite everything that gets thrown at them, they stand!

I know people like that, and I am full of admiration for them.

The next time you see a *krummholz* don't judge it in comparison to trees that grow in better climates. Give it a metaphorical tip of the hat for, heroically, being there at all.

Wednesday — July 3

THE writer Grenville Kleiser once said, "To live at this time is an inestimable privilege, and a sacred obligation devolves upon you to make right use of your opportunities."

Would you agree? Well, Kleiser did the majority of his writing in the run-up to World War I. Life was hardly a bed of roses back then, for anyone. But I imagine it was life itself, rather than the circumstances surrounding it, that he thought so highly of.

Circumstances will always change, sometimes for the better, sometimes for the worse, but life will always remain a wonderful gift. And, having received that gift, why would we do anything other than "make right use" of it?

Thursday — July 4

THESE days fewer people have gardens. For some it means a lot less work, but I am sure we all appreciate, and would miss, the delight of seeing new life break through the soil.

Whether we garden or not, we might all experience a very similar delight. Bishop Desmond Tutu explained how when he said, "We all blossom in the presence of one who sees the good in us and who can coax the best out of us."

Be that gardener.

Friday — July 5

CHARLIE CHAPLIN was best known for his wonderful comedy, but actually, he was a very thoughtful man and his words were every bit as powerful as his silent slapstick. In a speech he read out at his seventieth birthday party, he discussed what he had learned through growing older.

Talking of things that went wrong or confrontations, he said he no longer feared them like he once did. He seemed to suggest they were inevitable, but good things could come from them if we approached them in the right spirit. "Even stars collide, and out of their crashing new worlds are born."

Summer splendour.

Saturday — July 6

WHO doesn't like a sunrise? But the noonday sun is a different thing altogether.

That new venture we were setting out on, that promise or new start we have made, or even the difficult day in prospect, might begin hesitantly, with doubt and worry, but persevere. As that great thinker and writer Charles Dickens wrote, "The sun himself is weak when he first rises, and gathers strength and courage as the day gets on."

You might feel like a weak, watery sunrise at first, but shine on a while!

Sunday — July 7

IF you pray, how do you pray? If you look for instruction on the matter in the Bible you will find people kneeling, holding hands up to Heaven, even prostrating themselves on the ground. So, I suppose the place to get it right is in the heart, rather than in the physical position.

After decades of thinking it childish, I returned to how I was first taught – kneeling at the foot of the bed. The simple, child-like nature of it works well for me because it is humbling. And when I kneel down, my pride has to come down there with me.

How do you pray?

Monday — July 8

I LIKE the tale of the mother who, frustrated by her son's increasingly selfish behaviour, told him, "When you grow up, you're going to live in Havington rather than Givington!"

I imagine the boy was confused, but I am sure she would have explained.

Hopefully, he changed his ways and eventually made himself a home in Givington – which would also serve to make him a welcome visitor at Havington, should the need arise.

Tuesday — July 9

BASHO is a Japanese word that means "a place where one can feel at home and be oneself." The name has been applied to art galleries, cafés, even recovery centres. Places that are truly naturally *ibasho* are prized, and those set up to serve a specific therapeutic purpose are valuable, but people who are *ibasho* – people around whom we feel we can relax and truly be ourselves – ah, they are precious indeed.

What an honour it would be, if we could provide that feeling for others.

Wednesday — July 10

A YOUNG friend was on holiday in Florida – during a hurricane! Perusing the aftermath, he saw cars blown into gardens, sidings ripped off walls, and debris everywhere. But the pool enclosures in people's gardens were largely undisturbed. These structures usually have wood or metal frames covered in a fine mesh. Their purpose is mainly to keep bugs out of the swimming pool.

But the wind, no matter how strong, passes right through them.

We might deal with the storms in life in a similar fashion. Don't let them blow you over. Wait while they blow themselves out, let them pass through, and maybe go for a swim instead!

Thursday — July 11

SORROW. It touches every life at least once and our response is often to shun others and hide ourselves away. But John Kebble, an 18th-century churchman and poet, suggested the best remedy was actually to carry on with the daily round, suggesting that our everyday company would be a soothing balm.

In a beautiful couplet, he wrote:

"The herbs we seek to heal our woe,

Familiar by our pathway grow."

Friday — July 12

GREAT-AUNT LOUISA, in her diary, recounts being charmed by a day-dreaming three-year-old girl.

When asked by her smiling mother what she was thinking about, the little cherub replied, "Oh, stroking kittens. And puppies."

Louisa, who looked for learning opportunities in most things, went on to recall the hymnist Elizabeth Charles who wrote, "Let us only take care that, by the glance being turned inward, or strained onward, or lost in vacant reverie, we do not miss our turn of service, and pass by those to whom we might have been sent on an errand straight from God."

With a sweetness her great-niece, my own Lady of the House, also possesses, Louisa added, "Of course, stroking pets might also be seen as God's work – at least by the kittens and puppies!

Saturday — July 13

STEVE JOBS, the founder of Apple Inc., is supposed to have said, "The journey is the reward."

Legend has a king sending his three sons to the fabled city of Serendip in search of treasure, but it's what they learn on the journey that makes them wise rulers.

New goals are wonderful, but we should never be so focused on the goals that we neglect the rewards – the treasures – to be found along the way.

Sunday — July 14

ALISON is a student. She lives in a sparsely furnished flat in a tower block. Her view is mostly rooftops and sky. Rather than hang curtains over the one large window, she painted the wall around it like a camera, complete with hands holding it and a finger pressing the button to take a snap.

"Because," as she told me, "the sky is a new view every day."

She doesn't have much in her flat at the moment – but it is full of appreciation!

Friends for ever.

Monday — July 15

GIVING a speech at a high school graduation, the actress Sandra Bullock made an interesting point.

"You never remember the days you spent worrying."

Most of us have worried about a lot of things at different times, but how many of those days actually stick in your mind? Some few, perhaps. But days filled with joy? We remember them!

So, if you want a life worth remembering, then you might take a little more of Ms Bullock's advice from the same speech.

"Choose today, whether you are going to have a good day, or a great day." But don't worry!

Tuesday — July 16

THE chambered nautilus is a sea-creature that lives in a spiral shell. As it grows it adds ever-larger chambers to the spiral. For physician and poet Oliver Wendell Holmes it was a perfect metaphor for our spiritual development.

"Build thee more stately mansions, O my soul,

As the swift seasons roll."

He advised we make, "each new temple nobler than the last."

If we make today nobler (or simply better) than yesterday, and tomorrow nobler still, how "stately" will our lives become?

Wednesday — July 17

THISTLES can be noble plants, but they can also overgrow an area, making it impassable, and spread their seeds far and wide. Gardeners tend not to allow them into the areas they cultivate.

We might see our lives like gardens and pay them the same level of attention. Some of the "plants" that try to take root there might seem attractive at first, but eventually, they do a lot of damage.

We might also benefit from the wisdom of Frances Hodgson Burnett who, in her novel "The Secret Garden", wrote, "Where you tend a rose, my lad, a thistle cannot grow." Tend your life's roses.

Thursday — July 18

IN Ancient China the ruling families often claimed a "Heavenly mandate". The idea being that the gods granted them power and influence — so long as they ruled justly and morally. If they failed to be moral, then Heaven would withdraw that mandate and their power would fail.

It's a nice story, but what does it have to do with us and our lives?

Well, we, too, can claim a Heavenly mandate. Or, at least, we can live our lives by just and moral standards.

Will that make us emperors of China? Sorry, no.

Then what, I can imagine some asking, is the point? Surely it is better to play the world at its own game and take what we can get by whatever means we can.

Why not try both (if you must)? Live by this world's rules, then live by those heavenly rules.

And then tell me what difference it makes.

Friday — July 19

THE success or failure of almost every venture is usually ensured in the planning stage. Gloria Steinem, the journalist and political activist, was talking about the importance, and potential, of dreams when she wrote, "Dreaming, after all, is a form of planning."

And I thought back to a long list of frustrated teachers who told me off for dreaming in class.

If I could go back in time and assure them I was actually planning, would I?

Probably not.

Planning a trip to Mars, or how to dig an escape tunnel from the stationery cupboard all the way home, probably wasn't as important to my future as their plans for me to pass my exams.

But, still . . . when you think of all the wonderful, amazing, fantastical achievements that once were flights of fancy, perhaps we ought not to be so harsh with the dreamers.

Or, should I say, the planners?

Saturday — July 20

SOME are brown and some are blue,
They come in every kind of hue,
Some are large and some are small,
Some mystify and some enthrall.

Some are innocent and wide,
Some a secret seem to hide,
Some are young and some are old,
Some are shy and some are bold.

All creatures who have eyes to see,
Hold a special magic key,
For in life's complex mixing bowl,
Eyes are the windows of the soul.

– Brian H. Gent.

Sunday — July 21

THE Rabbi of Jabneh is a near mythical figure from Jewish history. He may have lived during and after the Roman destruction of Jerusalem. And yet, many of the words accredited to him then are still applicable today.

Discussing the different ways in which different people earned their living, he claimed that the priest's work was of no more value than the shepherd's, providing they both did whatever it was they did with their hearts directed towards Heaven.

What will you do today and which way will your heart be directed?

Monday — July 22

THESE days it seems there is a phone "app" for everything. "Wouldn't it be good," Matt said, "if there was an app that showed you the kindest moment of a person's life before we were nasty to them?"

Being nasty to people would, I am sure, quickly become a thing of the past if there was.

Tuesday — July 23

A WEARY friend said, "Sometimes I would just like to move somewhere new, where no-one knew me, and start again."

"What would you do differently?" I asked. "Because, surely, if you did all the same things in the new place, the same problems would still arise."

"Oh, I would do things very differently," he assured me.

"Then why not do them differently here?" I asked. "You would get all the benefits of your new ways, plus a whole lot of people would be amazed into the bargain."

So, he did. And they were.

Wednesday — July 24

TIME and motion studies, combined with computerisation, mean work is being done at ever increasing rates. That's all right for robots and those who work with them. But for the rest of us . . .

A century and a half ago the writer and philosopher Thomas Carlyle found something that let a worker do more in the same time, to persevere longer, and produce a higher quality product.

What was it? Singing while they worked!

If there's a chore you'd rather not do today, then don't avoid it. Face it with everything you need in the way of equipment. But, first of all, choose a song to sing as you do it.

Thursday — July 25

THE tradition may have begun on the Pont des Arts, a bridge over the River Seine. Lovers would inscribe their initials on padlocks, fasten them to the bridge, and throw the keys into the river.

Eventually, fearing for the integrity of the structure, city officials removed and took away 45 tonnes of padlocks. Eventually, the weight of all that extra iron might have brought the bridge down.

It's a nice thought that accumulated love can be a very powerful force!

Friday — July 26

TWO little boys in a playgroup were arguing over a pencil. Before the playleader could intervene, the pencil was snapped in two. The boy who had been trying to take the pencil was upset. The boy who had held the pencil first looked at the two pieces. One half was still useable. So, he sharpened the other half and gave it to the other boy. Now they both had a pencil.

I hope that child grows up to be a politician or a diplomat. The world could use more of that sort of thinking.

Saturday — July 27

A YOUNG friend is in training for a 10k run. Which is quite something as she had never run more than the length of a hockey field before. I saw her coming home one day and asked how the training session had gone. She said she felt terrible, walked half of it, and even sat on the kerb at one point.

"Wow!" I said. "That must really make you feel like giving up."

She looked amazed.

"Not at all!" she insisted. "Those are the times I need to overcome to get better. And now I've reached them!"

The first step in overcoming all our problems in life is getting to them. It's a victory in its own right.

Sunday — July 28

DOES it ever seem that problems from the past and worries for the future might rob today of all its joys? It probably happens to us all. Mary Frances Butts' charming little verse, published in 1898, might have been written in anticipation of our need for it.

"Build a little fence of trust around today.

Fill the space with loving work, and therein stay.

Look not through the sheltering bars upon tomorrow.

God will help thee bear what comes of joy or sorrow."

Monday — July 29

I STOOD entranced by the majestic sight of the horse-chestnut tree. It wasn't the spread or the colour of its leaves that caught my attention. It was the beautifully formed, but still small, "conkers" hanging from the branches. All of my childhood, conkers (the brown nuts inside the spiky green shells) have symbolised autumn.

Right now, autumn is a long time away, but of course, the seasons don't know about dates and calendars. The horse-chestnut tree reminded me that seasons don't begin, grow old, and die. They develop into their fullness and then they spend their time preparing for what must happen next.

Is there a lesson there for us?

Tuesday — July 30

H E looked like he'd walked a hard road. Several layers of ragged woollens separated him from the wind.

When I asked what the day ahead had in store, he said, "This is my day for being among the poor. I have some helping to do."

As we talked, I re-evaluated my idea of what "poor" was. It wasn't him, even though I had thought so moments before. It wasn't the people he helped, for they had a friend in him. Perhaps the real poor are the ones who seem to have everything, except a day in their diary for helping others.

Wednesday — July 31

I N an encouraging mood, President Theodore Roosevelt once said, "Believe you can, and you're halfway there!"

I do like that. But, it begins with you and me and only takes us halfway!

How about if we start off believing God can, and then adding our own efforts? That should take care of pretty much anything worth doing.

August

Thursday — August 1

ONE of my favourite poems (and paintings) is "La Belle Dame Sans Merci". I have heard different translations of the title. Some say it means "The Beautiful Lady Without Thanks", others that it is "The Beautiful Lady Without Mercy". The title isn't explained in the poem, although the title character, who is one of the fairy-folk, is quite implacable.

Regardless of translation, it struck me how much the words have in common. If we are thankful, we will generally be merciful, passing on our thanks in a practical way. If we feel we have nothing to be thankful for, we are less likely to be merciful.

Given the importance of those attitudes, let us appreciate the works of art and poetry for what they are but never follow the example of the "lady in the meads".

Let us always, rather, be with mercy, and with thanks.

Friday — August 2

THE slip of paper was still damp from the last shower. It was torn and I could find no clue as to whether it had been accidentally dropped or thrown to the wind in the hope of someone benefiting from it.

Judge nothing and you will be happy. Forgive someone and you will be happier. Love everything and you will be happiest.

I looked around the park at the various people there, and wondered who might need to read those words next.

I smoothed the "tract" out on the bench, preparing to leave it there.

In that moment, I loved the paper that bore the message, I loved the message, and I loved whoever had put them together and sent them out into the world.

A place to sit and stare.

Saturday — August 3

SIGNET rings, if they are worn at all these days, tend to be for decoration, but originally they had another purpose. The ring would bear a family crest – and a message!

When a letter was sealed with a blob of wax, the ring would be pressed into the wax. Thereafter, anyone seeing the letter would know which family was behind it – and how much authority or force might come after anyone tampering with it!

We no longer (most of us) seal letters with wax, but we all make an imprint on each day we live, and on the minds and hearts of each person we meet.

What message are you sending today?

Sunday — August 4

SINCE the days before science was even called science, back when it was just "magic", people have tried to transform base metals into precious metals. Lead into gold, for example; taking things that were relatively abundant and, through science or wizardry, making them more precious. Alchemy.

A wise friend recently brought all of that to mind when she said, "Do you know what the best kind of alchemy is? Turning hate into love."

I can think of no better way to make something precious.

Monday — August 5

A FRIEND buys and sells books for a living. From time to time he finds a rare one or one that can be rebound and sold for a profit. The other day, though, he was excited to tell me he had a 1953 edition of Sir Walter Scott's tale of chivalry and romance, "Ivanhoe".

"Is it worth anything?" I asked.

"I doubt it," he said, "but it's exactly the same as the one I had confiscated for reading it under the desk at school!"

A book that transports you to simpler, happier days – a rare find, indeed.

Tuesday — August 6

IREAD an informative article on gates. It was much more interesting than it sounds. It talked about great gates of the world, like the Brandenburg Gate in Germany and the ornamental gates outside Buckingham Palace, down to the ones at the end of our garden paths.

The question behind it was, did we use the gates in our lives to keep people safe, or to shut them out?

Gates do both, of course. But my favourite kind doesn't really do either.

My favourite gates are the ones we can lean on, so we can chat to passers-by, or contemplate the countryside, being neither in or out, just simply being.

Wednesday — August 7

DOUBTLESS the line came from the same rich and diverse Indian tradition my friend's family were a proud part of.

She had helped with a plan that needed to stay secret for a few days before, hopefully, delighting someone who was struggling. As we enjoyed the anticipation, she said, "When you plant a seed of kindness, it is you who blossoms."

I thought of the warm feeling in my stomach, the swelling of my heart, the width of my smile – and I could not deny it.

Thursday — August 8

IS there a purpose to friendship? I think most would see friendship as its own reward, a blessing complete in and of itself.

Would something so wonderful need a purpose?

Perhaps not, but it would surely be an added bonus if, as well as everything else friendship had going for it, there was also a purpose behind it.

In the 19th century Cardinal John Henry Newman said, "The love of our private friends is the only preparatory exercise for the love of all men."

Friday — August 9

SOME of my most frustrating days are those when I don't have time to walk. It might be walking to get somewhere, walking the dogs, or just going nowhere in particular. A good wander takes me away from distractions and gives my unconscious mind time to tidy up the issues clamouring for my attention.

The exercise is good for me. And the views, the breeze on my cheek, the chance to splash in the occasional puddle when no-one is looking, all refresh my soul.

All of which is a long way of expressing what the Romans put into two words. "Solvitur ambulando" – it is solved by walking.

Saturday — August 10

SHE was a Chinese student, trying to make ends meet in the UK. From time to time the Lady of the House and I would help in little ways.

She must have appreciated having friends who were closer than half the world away. When it came time to leave she presented us with a card. Inside was a strip of postage stamps with paintings of flowers and Chinese characters on them.

I was confused until she said, "It is something of my home. For you."

Could we ever give, or receive, a more heartfelt gift?

Sunday — August 11

TWO good-sized plums grew on David's tree. He picked them, washed them, and ate one of them. It tasted so sweet and delicious he cut the other one into four pieces so his children could share the experience.

They thought it was all right. A plum. Nothing special.

"But they hadn't planted the tree," David told me. "They hadn't cared for it, and waited three years for that first fruit."

What we invest in anything plays a big part in how sweet it tastes! Worth remembering when we're feeling impatient.

Monday — August 12

IF you lived in an enclosed environment, like a convent or a monastery, you would hope everyone was even-tempered and obliging. And wouldn't that be nice in ordinary lives as well?

Bernard of Clairvaux, a monk, thought every monastery should have at least one "awkward and ill-tempered" person in it.

Learning to deal with them wisely brings astonishing results.

So, let us value the contrary ones for what they bring out in us, all the while trying not to be one of them!

Tuesday — August 13

THOSE of us who have gathered a goodly collection of years often have cause to look back on particular seasons with regret. We wonder where we went wrong, why we wasted valuable time on pointless detours. Why, we ask, were we not more intent on striving for something good?

St Theresa of Avila gave us a very convenient excuse when she said, "To reach for something good it is very useful to have gone astray – and thus acquire experience."

The wisdom that, hopefully, comes with age will understand it was more of a truth than an excuse.

Wednesday — August 14

YOU may not have heard of Robert Lynd, but a reviewer, writing in 1941, describes him as the pre-eminent essayist of his generation and his book the perfect antidote to "the dinginess of war".

What did he write about? Well, springtime and galoshes, kissing on stage, wildflowers, happiness, chickens, wishful thinking, lemons, haircuts and clip-on ties.

In the depths of war! And every essay a guaranteed grin.

It's a much under-appreciated blessing that in times of national trial or personal difficulty there will usually be some equivalent of Mr Lynd around to draw our attention back (with a smile) to the things that make life worth living.

Thursday — August 15

HOW do we be holy? For many it seems an unattainable goal. Others think we need some dramatic spiritual encounter to make us so.

But it is within all our grasp! The English clergyman Edward Pusey described it this way: "Holiness does not consist of doing uncommon things. It consists of doing common things in an uncommon way."

That "uncommon way" is, of course, how God would have it done. Learning to do the ordinary things in our lives that way is the surest path to holiness or, at the very least, a better life.

Friday — August 16

SOME imaginative individual once said, "Laughter is the sound of your soul dancing."

It's an enchanting notion and, given all the different ways people do laugh, it might be fun to wonder what style your own soul dances in. Does your chuckle, snicker, chortle or all-out belly-laugh mean that your soul is a tap-dancer, a mosher, an American-smoother, a salsa-dancer or a waltzer?

In the end, it doesn't matter. So long as you laugh.

So long as your soul dances.

Saturday — August 17

IBOUGHT a book dedicated to the Small Pilgrim Places Network and just had to look it up. It seems that local chapters of the Network, up and down the country, are dedicated to finding "spaces for pondering, breathing, meditating, praying and simply being."

They tend to be relatively unknown, quiet, unpretentious places where the Divine, somehow, feels closer.

It occurred to me I could happily spend many years exploring a network like that. But, for those of us who can't, there is always the option of finding such places in our own lives.

We can always be pilgrims in our own neighbourhood.

THERE'S light at the end of the tunnel,
We often hear folk say,
When we feel beset by problems
And life gets in the way.

The path ahead seems cheerless,
A lonely, rocky ride,
So look around for travellers,
Journeying at your side

And reach into that darkness,
With your eyes fixed on the light,
To take the hand of someone
Who also shares your plight.

There's light at the end of the tunnel,
No need to lose your way.
Let's travel through together,
Into the bright new day.

— Linda Brown.

Monday — August 19

THE Scottish obstetrician James Young Simpson faced opposition as he attempted to introduce pain-relieving anaesthesia into the process of child-birth.

He apparently said, "I feel that the greater the good I can accomplish . . . the greater will always be the temporary blame heaped on me."

The important word there – one that also applies to our own attempts to do good – is "temporary".

People always oppose change, but if what we are trying to do is truly good it will outlast every negative thing said about it.

The criticism will blow away in the wind.

The good will remain.

Happy birthday!

Tuesday — August 20

"PEOPLE are just too kind," Mandy said, dabbing a happy tear. She had received a gift for her new baby from a friend of her dad – someone she had never met.

It wasn't the only gift her baby had received from people who hadn't met her.

I don't think it's the case that people are too kind. I think kindness is the default position for most of us.

Sometimes we just need something as pure and innocent as a newborn baby to remind us of that.

Wednesday — August 21

IMAGINE if good deeds were done for reward. What reward would be enough? Most good souls are content with the notion they made something better, or someone happier, but the Talmud suggests that, "When a person does a good deed, when he or she doesn't have to, God looks down and smiles and says, 'For this moment alone, it was worth creating the world'."

Such is the value people in bygone times placed on kindness. Why should we value it any less?

And wouldn't that be the most beautiful reward ever?

Thursday — August 22

THIS life has many problems, Lord,
Some great and others small,
But through the years of doubts and fears
You see and know them all.
But there are compensations, too,
With happiness to share,
With love which grows and knows no bounds
Around us everywhere.

– Iris Hesselden.

Friday — August 23

JOHN was in a café. Deciding to do a good deed, he offered to pay for the meal of a poor-looking woman. She laughed, then politely declined.

Cringing, he went back to his own lunch. Before he left the waitress explained that the poor-looking woman was, actually, quite wealthy. Touched by his offer, she had left enough money to pay for several lunches for whoever might need them.

Good deeds! They might not work out as we would like – but they generally work out!

Saturday — August 24

LEWIS CARROLL once wrote, "It's no use going back to yesterday because I was a different person then."

We all enjoy a wander down Memory Lane, but we are different people now. If we could go back we would no longer see those things through the eyes of innocence and inexperience. We might want to do things better (which, of course, we can't).

But there is one useful, practical thing to be done down that lane. We might stroll along it long enough to forgive our younger selves for the mistakes we made when we did not know what we know now.

And, having forgiven, we come back home again – forgiven.

Sunday — August 25

THE evangelist D.L. Moody travelled around the world, meeting all sorts of people. Doubtless, some were less civil than others. He would have been heckled at more than a few meetings.

However, there was one person he had regular battles with. He wrote, "I have more trouble with D.L. Moody than any other man I know!"

The spiritual battle might seem to be between believers and non-believers. But, if the believer takes their faith seriously they will have enough on their hands dealing with themselves.

Monday — August 26

LOVE is a wonderful thing, but it surely has limits and it would be impossible to love the whole world?

Not according to the novelist Dostoyevsky, who wrote the following:

Love all God's creation, both the whole and every grain of sand. Love every leaf, every ray of light. Love the animals, love the plants, love each separate thing.

If thou love each thing thou wilt perceive the mystery of God in all . . . until thou come at last to love the whole world with a love that will then be all embracing and universal.

Tuesday — August 27

WHEN Paul's friend was diagnosed with cancer he went to every appointment with him, waited through the treatments, and helped him celebrate at the end of it.

Once, sitting waiting, Paul told a nurse he wished he could do more for his friend.

She said, "You're here for him, letting him know he isn't alone, keeping him cheery. You're doing angels' work!"

"It seems it doesn't take much to do angels' work," Paul told me. "You don't even need wings – just a hand to hold out!"

Wednesday — August 28

ON the wall of my hall hangs a framed version of the old saying, "No act of kindness, no matter how small, is ever wasted."

It was a gift of appreciation from . . . I know not who.

The phrase might seem a little clichéd these days, but it is attributed to Aesop, of fables fame, and he lived five hundred years before Christ.

So, that little saying has been around for two and a half centuries. And still, no-one has been able to refute it.

That's all the proof I need of its truth.

Rolling hills.

Dorset, England.

Thursday — August 29

THE Bag Ladies are a group of retired women who collect plastic bags. They clean them, cut them into strips, wind them together to make "plastic yarn", and crochet them into comfortable, warm and free blankets.

Then they donate the blankets to homeless people and disaster victims.

Now, it would be better not to have so many disposable plastic bags in the community. And it would definitely be better for people not to be homeless. Society – people – mess up. Mistakes are made.

But it restores my faith that for every mistake that's made, for every time mankind goes wrong, there are people like the Bag Ladies, working quietly and inventively to turn that wrong thing into a wonderful thing!

Friday — August 30

AFTER a tsunami hit Japan, leaving thousands homeless, a project was set up to help restore communities. As a part of that, people searched through the wreckage for pieces of broken porcelain, pottery and glass. They sanded the fragments down, set them in pieces of jewellery, and sold them across the world to raise funds.

It shows us the value of that place we each call home, when even the tiniest shard of it might justifiably take the place of precious stones.

Saturday — August 31

WE'VE all seen films where lovers share a kiss knowing it will be their last. So poignant! It is usually only in the losing of things that we fully appreciate their worth to us. What would life be like if we had that level of appreciation all the time?

"Look thy last on all things lovely," Walter de la Mare wrote. In other words, appreciate them like you might never see them again.

As for those things unlovely, feel free to pay them considerably less attention.

September

Sunday — September 1

PRAYING had long been a part of Elizabeth's life. It became more so after her husband died and old age brought her the usual infirmities.

Shopping in the supermarket one day, she saw a big box of washing powder for a price that, on her limited budget, was too good to ignore. So, she bought it, but she hadn't gone twenty steps along the road before she realised it would be too heavy for her. She stopped, and asked God for help.

I'd already walked past, but something prompted me to turn. When I asked if I could help, I heard her mutter, "Thank you, Lord."

I can't say for sure that it was God who turned me around. But, I can't say it wasn't, either. What I can say for sure is that Elizabeth asked – and she was answered!

Monday — September 2

I WAS reminded of an old Chinese curse by a comment on the life of a 14th-century gentleman. The curse goes, "May you live in interesting times". Of course, times tend to be most interesting when they tend to be most turbulent!

Sir John de Stonor was Chief Justice of the Common Pleas under two kings. The first king was deposed by the second one, but Sir John's work was so valued he was invited to simply keep on doing it. A biographer noted that, "the dullness of the record of Sir John's career is perhaps the best indication we can obtain as to the excellence of his good qualities."

Interesting times tend to be made so by mistakes and man's baser desires. When good men and women do good work and live in good times the historical interest might be minimal, but those are the lives to live, and those are the times to live in.

Tuesday — September 3

IT was Nathan's first day at school. He'd been for a couple of visits and was looking forward to it, but Mum was still emotional. The thought of her baby becoming a schoolboy was all a bit much for her. When the school bus arrived, Nathan bounded excitedly up the steps with his friends. He turned to wave goodbye and noticed the tears on his mother's cheeks.

"Don't be sad, Mum," he shouted. "Maybe you can ride on the school bus one day, too!"

One situation, but two very different points of view.

We ought to remember before we agree or disagree with anyone to make sure we both see the situation the same way.

Wednesday — September 4

SINCE the beginnings of humanity, men and women have imparted their wisdom to whoever would listen. The best of it was passed, orally, on down the generations. After writing was invented people started recording the words of the wise ones, in clay, then on parchment, then on paper, and, these days, digitally.

So, it might be fair to say there are many, many libraries-worth of wisdom accumulated in the world. It would be a brave man who attempted to condense them. But Alexander Dumas did just that when he wrote, "All human wisdom is summed up in two words: wait and hope."

Wisely, I decided to wait before agreeing, and I hope he is correct!

Thursday — September 5

FACED with some less than pleasant events on the news, my friend Rev. Hugh paused, thought for a moment and then said, "While the ugliness is so often confrontational and in your face, the beauty often hides, waiting for you to find it."

What can I add to such wisdom? Just that the beauty is well worth the search. And, really, why would we spend our time looking for anything else?

Friday — September 6

TIME now for the harvest,
The gifts of fruit and grain,
For all the blessings, great and small
Bestowed by sun and rain.
And time to think of other gifts,
So many we receive,
For love and hope and thoughtfulness
And all we can achieve.
A time to think of other lands
And send a healing prayer,
To reach out far across the earth
And show the world we care.

— Iris Hesselden.

Saturday — September 7

THE poet Jalalludin Rumi, who lived in Persia in the 13th century, wrote, "In this earth, in this soil, in this pure field, let us not plant any seed other than seeds of love and compassion."

Pretty, isn't it? Now, imagine we changed it around a little, made it, "In this heart or mine, in this child, in this passing stranger . . ."

If, given the choice, we would only plant good seeds in the fertile soil, why would we plant anything else in each other's lives?

Sunday — September 8

ANCIENT Chinese wisdom suggests that, "If you are patient in one moment of anger, you will escape a hundred days of sorrow." Viktor Frankl, the Austrian psychiatrist and concentration camp survivor, suggested that our happiness, or otherwise, is decided in the split-second between the action and the reaction.

How do we find that patience? What do we do in that split second? How about, in those critical moments, we say to ourselves, "Thy will be done, Lord"? And ask Him how He would have you react.

The end result is bound to be a better one!

Monday — September 9

I READ a somewhat flippant piece of advice that went, "If you are being run out of town, get out in front and turn it into a parade!"

Now, I doubt if any amount of baton twirling and cheering would turn that sort of crowd into anything positive. But one person can change the mood of a group, for the better or the worse.

If you find yourself in a group situation that has a less than positive feel about it, be the mood-changer.

Strike up the band! Get that parade going!

Tuesday — September 10

THE picture was called "The Importance Of A Single Tree". The tree itself wasn't all that imposing, but it was green and its branches spread out for about twenty feet in every direction, providing a wide circle of shade on an otherwise parched landscape. And that shade was completely full of goats seeking refuge from the harsh noonday sun. One tree sheltering perhaps 80 goats.

We can, hopefully, do likewise, so that people look at how we live, how we treat others, and comment on the importance of a single life. Be a shelter for many, if you can. But maybe do it for people . . . and plant some other trees for the goats!

Wednesday — September 11

BOARDING the train to Durham, I found myself sitting across from a gran and granddaughter on a girls' day out. They chatted happily for most of the trip, but when they weren't talking, ah!

When the girl wasn't talking she looked at the beautiful scenery. When the woman wasn't talking she looked at her granddaughter.

If there is one thing more wonderful than being loved," I muttered, "it's loving."

She heard me and replied, "You know what that feels like."

Happily, I do!

Thursday — September 12

FAITH BALDWIN, a novelist who wrote in the first half of the 20th century, wrote, "Time is a dressmaker, specialising in alterations."

Life is a series of changes. Imagine we went to a dressmaker, or tailor, at regular intervals and insisted they only worked to the first set of measurements? What heights of style and sophistication might we never achieve?

Embrace the alterations, rejoice in the new things each season (in fashion and in life) brings.

Let the dressmaker – and time – work their wonders. Appreciate them and enjoy them.

Friday — September 13

SHAKESPEARE created many of the expressions we use in conversation these days. I don't know if he came up with the phrase "We have seen better days" but he certainly wrote it down. And I have heard many weary souls utter it recently, as if they thought the whole world was on an inexorably downward spiral.

But, given that each day begins full to the brim with possibilities, we cannot deny that each new one might be a better day than any we have seen so far. If only we will help make it so.

When looking for better days, don't look backwards with a sigh, look forward with a smile and determination in your heart.

Saturday — September 14

GEORGE DU MAURIER, the 19th-century author and cartoonist, had an interesting take on one of our favourite emotions.

"Happiness," he wrote, "is like time and space; we make and measure it ourselves; it is as fancy, as big, as little, as wide as you please."

If we could tailor-make our happinesses – and I'm not convinced we don't – I would have most of mine understated and relaxed, with the occasional one that lights up the sky! How about you? Which style of happiness would Sir or Madam prefer?

Sunday — September 15

I DO not know her name. She is described as "a poor Methodist woman" living in the 18th century. She made a living from needlework and her cottage was lit by candles.

So, no electricity, no car, no central heating, no TV. Not the smallest fraction of the electrical goods and conveniences we have these days. But was she happy?

"I rejoice in who I am," she is recorded as saying, "a creature capable of loving God, and who, as long as God lives, must be happy. I get up and look for a while out the window and gaze at the moon and the stars, the work of an almighty hand. I think of the grandeur of the universe and then sit down and think myself one of the happiest beings in it."

I do not know her name. But I know she was the loving daughter of a loving God.

Monday — September 16

LARKS are known for their sudden and speedy ascents to great heights. This speed and agility has always made them difficult for hunters to catch. In the mind of the great thinker and father of modern literature Francois Rabelais, though, it also made them a fine example of how to find good in even the worst of situations.

"If the sky falls," he wrote, "one may, at least, hope to catch larks!"

Tuesday — September 17

SOMEONE compared a smile to a million pounds in the bank. "Unfortunately," he added, "some people seem to have lost their cheque book." In other words, they had a great resource at their disposal, but they never used it.

Think of the obstacles that are reduced by a smile, the happiness that is gifted by a smile, and the pleasure that smiling generates in our own heart. How much would someone have to pay you to give that up? A smile is a priceless asset, but only if we use it!

Morning song.

Wednesday — September 18

AN Italian proverb says, "The comforter's head never aches." If that were true then I imagine people would be clamouring to be comforters. I think it is a little more complicated. Often those who comfort have suffered in the past. And they may do so again. But I am sure they don't suffer while they are comforting, while they are solely focused on another.

Of course, that's just my opinion. Do me a favour. Try it, and tell me what you think.

Thursday — September 19

A GARDENER found himself battling against a particularly tenacious type of weed. He pulled them up, they grew again. He sat stones on them, they grew elsewhere. Different weed-killers were put to work. They failed!

He phoned the local parks department, looking for expert advice. He described the weed and all the various ways he had tried to eradicate it. When he finished, the parks man said simply, "I suggest you learn to love it."

Sometimes we come up against situations, or people, we can do nothing about. We can ignore them, or learn to love them. Loving them won't make them any nicer but it will make our lives less frustrating, and make us better people into the bargain

Friday — September 20

I DO like seeing the blossom on the trees. It really gives my soul a lift. Of course, at this time of year the blossoms have long been scattered by the winds.

The Japanese writer and monk Yoshida Kenko wrote, "Blossoms are scattered by wind, and the wind cares nothing, but the blossoms of the heart no wind can reach."

As the winds pick up and the leaves begin to fall, cherish the blossoms of the heart. And share them with others. That way blossom season might last all year round.

Saturday — September 21

THE image the Puritans had of seeing pleasure as a sin and never cracking a smile is probably nonsense, as most stereotypes are. But there are plenty of people around these days who are too busy taking life seriously to enjoy it very much.

The author Robert Louis Stevenson had some words for them.

If your morals make you dreary, depend on it, they are wrong.

In a world where puppies chase their tails, where babies gurgle, where young folk fall in love (and old folk show them how to do it properly), where sunsets leave people speechless, and children sing for the sake it, any system of morals or beliefs that doesn't have joy as an important part of it just isn't trying hard enough.

Sunday — September 22

I OFTEN wondered about the Bible verse where Jesus says, "Do not resist the evil man." Then I read Carl Jung, who said, "What you resist, persists."

Evil things, by their nature, create conflict. If we oppose them with conflict we are, in fact, feeding them, helping them to persist. I'm not suggesting we ignore such people, but that we don't fight them with the weapons they are prepared for and well versed in using.

How about we take them by surprise, opposing them – and perhaps restoring them – by employing a different "weapon", the one suggested by Jesus when He said, "Love your enemies."

Monday — September 23

LIFE is like . . ." I have heard many examples of things life might be compared to. The writer Ralph Waldo Emerson went for a more blanket approach – in more ways than one.

"We do not live an equal life, but one of contrasts and patchwork; now a little joy, then a sorrow, now a sin, then a generous or brave action."

A patchwork quilt! That's what life is like!

Tuesday — September 24

HAVE you ever tried to write poetry? I have. And I can't, though I enjoy reading it and I admire the skill that goes into it. Why do I even mention this? Because it's good to have some limitations.

"When power leads man towards arrogance, poetry reminds him of his limitations," John F. Kennedy said. "When power narrows the area of man's concern, poetry reminds him of the richness and diversity of his existence. When power corrupts, poetry cleanses."

Wonderful, insightful thoughts. But you might notice that, even though he was the most powerful man in the world in his time, Kennedy couldn't make them rhyme!

It's nice that we have something in common.

Wednesday — September 25

THE 14th-century poet Hafiz addressed a class of students with these words: "The subject tonight is love. And for tomorrow night as well. As a matter of fact, I know of no better topic for us to discuss until we die."

Isn't that a wonderful thought? But imagine we put it into practice; imagine if every conversation we had was, in some way, about love. Would that be a challenge, or easy? Perhaps try it for a week. And then another one.

Imagine what a difference changing how we spoke would make to our lives – and the lives of everyone we spoke to!

Thursday — September 26

PRAYER is such a personal thing and can be applied to almost every situation. So how could there ever be such a thing as a perfect prayer?

Gotthold Ephraim Lessing, who was one of the leading figures of the Enlightenment in the 18th century, thought there was.

What was it?

"A simple grateful thought raised to Heaven," he wrote, "is the most perfect prayer."

The heavens above.

Friday — September 27

HE had been gently mocking me for my optimism. He may have been a little too full of the party spirit when he hugged me and said, "I hope the sun never stops shining for you! And if it does I hope the moon makes up for it!"

As he walked away, I called out, "What does that even mean?"

"I dunno!" he shouted back. And off he went, laughing to himself.

Perhaps he meant there are different ways to look at things, different ways to understand the purpose behind it all; perhaps even that those of a less sunny disposition might still find beauty in the world.

Or perhaps I'm just being too optimistic again.

But it's a beautiful line all the same. Don't you think so?

Saturday — September 28

AS a fund-raiser for motor neurone treatment and research the late, great comedian Jerry Lewis raised a phenomenal two and a half billion dollars in his lifetime. Add that to all the years spent making people laugh and it's not a bad legacy.

Of course, he knew lots of the biggest names in showbiz and he asked them for help along the way. Many of them appeared on his annual fund-raising telethon and he was grateful for their time and efforts.

Writing to Frank Sinatra to thank him for one such appearance, Lewis couldn't find words big enough to express his appreciation.

But, even in thanking Sinatra for doing him a favour, he still asked for another one. He asked that the great singer ask him for help sometimes, "and let me have some of the joy I see you get from the good things you do!"

We aren't supposed to boast of the good things we do, and I'm sure Frank Sinatra didn't, but surely it does no harm to delight in them.

In fact, as Jerry Lewis discovered, it might encourage more people to join us in doing those good things.

Sunday — September 29

Do you ever doubt yourself? I think most of us do at one time or another. That's not what matters, though. What matters is what we do with, and around, those doubts.

Sir Richard Eyre has had a long and notable career on stage, in television, in the movies, and in opera. As a young actor, he doubted his own ability to convince an audience so he moved into directing and never looked back.

For ever surrounded by artistic, creative people, he says, "I can't think of anyone I admire who isn't fuelled by self-doubt. It's an essential ingredient. It's the grit in the oyster."

Self-doubt. It isn't pleasant, but it's very often what drives us to try harder and do better.

And, of course, that annoying piece of grit in the oyster eventually becomes a pearl.

Monday — September 30

OH, next time I am passing . . ."
Have you said those words today?
Is there something that you mean to do when next you
pass this way?
Such as take a path you've often seen and wanted to explore,
Or climb a gate that leads to fields with meadow flowers galore?
Or follow signs, maybe, to places that you've never been –
To sights you've often heard about but somehow never seen.
Or have you said those words to friends, intending to drop by,
Yet there's never quite the time to stop, although you meant
to try?
Because there's always "next time", though you can't be sure
of when,
Who knows what life may bring, or if you'll pass this way again?
There's no time like the present. Think, and maybe make a vow:
Don't put it off till next time. Do it this time; do it now.

– Emma Canning.

October

Tuesday — October 1

I **HELD** the bird in my hand. It tried desperately to flap, but my fingers held the wings to its side. I could feel its heart beating frantically.

I waited, holding it firmly, but not too tightly. Gradually, the little thing's heart-rate slowed down. Then I could relax my fingers a little and undo the fishing line tangled around its legs. Once free, I set it on the grass. It flapped a few times, then took to the sky, free and unencumbered.

It's often the same when trying to help people. The first part of the battle is to get close to them.

The second part is to assure them you mean no harm. And then you get to help.

Wednesday — October 2

*C***AN** *you spare a moment*
Throughout a busy day,
To chat to someone lonely
You meet along your way?

So many folk are lonely
And need a little care,
A word or two of comfort
You could so kindly spare;

And by your understanding,
The little things you've done,
You'll make the world much brighter
And a far less lonely one!

– Elizabeth Gozney.

Thursday — October 3

I HAVE heard the story of the long struggle to invent the lightbulb told in many ways. Usually it involves Thomas Edison saying something like, "We haven't failed. We have simply found a thousand ways that don't work."

My favourite version of the tale has Jimmy, a homeless boy Edison gave shelter to, dropping the latest hand-made bulb and seeing it shatter on the floor. Edison, who might justifiably have been furious, put his hand on the boy's shoulder and said, "The thing about mistakes, Jimmy, is that they needn't be permanent."

How did that approach work out? How many working lightbulbs do you have in your home?

Friday — October 4

IT'S a modern saying, by our old friend A. Nonymous, that has the potential, I think, to become a fully-fledged proverb and be passed on through the ages.

"If you dig someone else out of their troubles," the saying goes, "you will have found a place to bury your own."

Now, it's a foregone conclusion that when we help others, we also help ourselves. And it would be a shame to leave that hole sitting empty!

Saturday — October 5

WE watch films and read books and some of us quietly hope we might do the noble, inspirational, brave, understanding, kind, or self-sacrificing thing the hero or heroine does. And, most likely, we could. Human beings are capable of wonderful acts, but we tend to save those wonderful acts for extreme situations and rare occasions. And, sometimes, those never come!

Why? If we are capable of being wonderful at those times – and we are – why don't we do it more often? It would be a more exciting book if the characters did that and a more fulfilling life if we did.

Sunday — October 6

A "SEEKER" is usually someone searching for God or spiritual enlightenment. Some people spend their whole lives seeking. But not Henry. "I'm not a seeker," he told me. "I'm a finder. After decades of wondering about God, I decided to live as if He was there. And when I did, I found Him everywhere!"

As it says in the Book of John, "Through him all things were made." Perhaps we all ought to focus less on seeking and more on finding. He is there to be found. Everywhere!

Monday — October 7

HOW much real, shout-out-loud joy do your possessions, your health, your relationships, bring you on an average day? Most of us, if we have these things, or acquire them, pretty soon start to take them for granted.

Now imagine they were taken away from you. And then given back. Might you punch the air in celebration, shout in delight, or say a heart-felt prayer of thanks?

The things won't have changed. We will just have been reminded of how much we really value them.

Which also reminds me of the words of a Greek philosopher from ancient times: "He is a man of sense who does not grieve for what he does not have – but rejoices in what he does have!"

Tuesday — October 8

IN some hospitals people recovering from certain operations, or who may be unsteady on their feet, are given a bright yellow wristband. To the medical staff the band says, "Watch this person carefully. They are at risk of falling. Help them get from place to place."

Falls may be physical, spiritual or emotional, but the nature of life leaves us all at risk of falling. We could do a lot worse, as a people, than to watch each other in a caring manner, be prepared to catch our neighbour when they stumble, and help everyone we meet get to where they are going.

Wednesday — October 9

AGGIE used to enjoy sharing salacious tales of people doing things they shouldn't. Then word reached her of something nasty she was supposed to have said, but hadn't! Realising half the town must have heard the rumour, she also realised that she had done the same to others in the past.

So, these days, she indulges in "anti-gossip", seeing how many good things she can find out about her neighbours and spreading that about.

"Strangely," Aggie said, "the word spreads a little slower, but when it finally gets back to the person concerned the glow on their face is worth the effort!"

Thursday — October 10

THE world often seems split between those who are romantically inclined and those of a more cynical nature.

The actor Jeff Bridges said, "I always think that cynics are really romantics who have been hurt some time in their lives and have put up this cynical mask to protect themselves."

So, actually, it seems the world is full of romantics – and people who just need more real romance in their lives.

Friday — October 11

SARA TEASDALE, a poet who lived between the great wars, wrote of an encounter with a philosopher. The man was ninety-two, but had the sparkling eyes of a child.

She asked him how he managed to keep joy burning in his eyes despite the frailty of his body.

His answer was simple – as all great words of wisdom tend to be. He said, "I make the most of all that comes, and the least of all that goes."

That's advice we might follow at any age, but the sooner we start the brighter, I imagine, the joy will shine.

Saturday — October 12

SUCCESS comes in different shapes and sizes. It might be getting into that dress, or scoring that goal, or closing that business deal. But there is one form of it we can all achieve.

The poet, novelist and civil-rights activist Maya Angelou described it like this – "If you can find it in your heart to care for somebody else, you will have succeeded."

Sunday — October 13

HAVE you heard of "But first" syndrome? It's when the dog needs walking, but first you need a coffee. You want to phone a lonely friend, but first you take a nap. The children want you to play, but first you have a programme to watch. All too often our best intentions disappear into the "but first" zone.

If you want to achieve more, to do the things you know you ought to, try this. Decide what needs doing, but first make it an offering to God. Then make it the best offering you can!

Monday — October 14

I HAD a dream of earth and sky,
Of soft clouds high above;
A dream of peace and happiness,
A dream of joy and love.

And in my dream the world was calm
With hope for everyone,
And all creation sighed and smiled:
A new time had begun.

I had a dream that life was good
And hurt was far away,
And we went forward, hand in hand.
Please share my dream today!

– Iris Hesselden.

A safe pair of hands.

Tuesday — October 15

DO you have a best friend? Some would find it difficult to decide who was best out of a large group of good friends. Others may be very happy with one friend who, by default, becomes their best friend. But how do you decide? What defines a best friend?

The car manufacturer Henry Ford had a definition I can find no fault with.

"My best friend is the one who brings out the best in me."

It's not about what they do for you. It's about what you become because they are your friend.

Wednesday — October 16

WOULDN'T it be fun (and possibly a little worrying) if there was some sort of gadget or mechanism we could use to attract new friends? I wonder how much one of those would cost.

But an Indian wise man suggested we already have one.

"There is a magnet in your heart that will attract true friends," he said. "That magnet is unselfishness; thinking of others first."

It seems we don't have to pay anything for the "gadget", that "magnet". We just need to use it.

Thursday — October 17

TO educate her daughters, Mum split an apple and showed them the seeds. She explained how each seed could grow into a tree that might grow thousands of apples in its lifetime.

The seeds went into pots. Eventually, they were planted in the garden. But the one belonging to Little Sister was planted in the shade. It grew at a slower pace than Big Sister's. It got a blight.

Then cats used it as a scratching post. A cousin fell on it.

I prepared to commiserate. But then Big Sister laughed.

"Ask her which tree grows the sweetest apples now."

Little Sister just smiled.

Friday — October 18

THE writer Richard Jefferies, who was known for his descriptions of English rural life, found winter an oddly joyful time.

"This is the only profit of frost," he wrote, "the pleasure of winter: to conquer cold and to feel braced and strengthened by that whose province is to wither and destroy. Thus, we make of cold – life's enemy – life's renewer."

Never forget each difficulty brings with it an opportunity to overcome it; each challenge that would bring us down also gives us the opportunity to rise up, using it as a stepping stone.

Saturday — October 19

AN elderly lady became a local celebrity after she used a marionette that looks just like her to feed squirrels in the park. As well as being cute, it saves her bending down. The squirrels probably like it because, as well as carrying nuts, the marionette is about their size. Despite her aches, she found an ingenious way to get down to their level.

If you would help others – humans or squirrels – don't bestow your largesse from above. Find a way to meet them face to face, where they live, at their level. You will understand them, and the value of your kindness, better.

And that's not just me being nuts!

Sunday — October 20

AN experienced hillwalker set up camp while his friend explored. Minutes later the friend staggered back bruised and dishevelled.

"It was a snake! A black snake!"

"Black snakes aren't dangerous." the experienced man said.

"They are if they give you such a fright you fall over a cliff!"

All too often it's our fears rather than the reality of our situation that do the damage. Perhaps that, and the fact that God watches over us, is why the Bible tells us so often, "Do not fear."

Monday — October 21

THERE is an Indian legend that shows how great things are accomplished by ordinary people. A sparrow's eggs fell from the nest into a river and rolled into the sea. Distraught, the sparrow set itself the task of drinking the whole sea to recover its eggs!

Other small birds watched in amazement as she began her impossible task. Larger birds, seeing the small birds, gathered around to see what the fuss was about. Eventually, the attention of Garuda, a giant eagle, was attracted. But Garuda was more than simply a bird; she carried the Lord Vishnu on her back. Vishnu, seeing the little sparrow's efforts, commanded the sea to return her eggs.

A great thing was accomplished because an ordinary bird refused to give up.

Tuesday — October 22

WULLIE built oil rigs. He spent his working days either in waterproofs or denims and a yellow "hard-hat" was ever-present. He smelled of gas burners and spent welding rods.

But when lunchtime came he opened his locker, hung a canvas on the door and painted seascapes.

I thought of Wullie when I read these words by the novelist Alice Walker. "Whenever you create beauty around you, you are restoring your soul."

The same applies when you arrange flowers, decorate a nursery, sing. Create beauty. Your soul will feel the benefit!

Wednesday — October 23

THERE'S an old Arabian proverb that, translated, goes along the lines of, "If you have much, give of your wealth. If you have little, give of your heart."

Beautiful, wise words. To which I add that if you have a loving, inclusive, generous heart, then you still have "much", no matter what you have in your bank account. And any time you give of it, you still give something precious!

Thursday — October 24

INDIVIDUALS, and even politicians, occasionally hark back to "golden ages", when life was more innocent, people were happier and the world was a kinder place.

Nostalgia is a fine thing, but to suggest such times are bygone implies they aren't here now, and won't be here in the future. But that is too beautiful a dream to let go of; to assume we can't have it in our lives.

The great theologian Augustine of Hippo would have agreed. He wrote, "If we live good times, the times are also good. As we are, such are the times."

Friday — October 25

THE mood changed – then changed again! The writer G.K. Chesterton had been enjoying an afternoon in the English countryside, sketching with chalks on brown paper. Until, that is, he realised he had no white chalk, without which his efforts would be for nothing.

He sank to the grass. But moments later he jumped up, laughing. He had been sitting on a massive chalk deposit. All he needed to do was break a bit off!

Saturday — October 26

IN 1845, Henry David Thoreau moved into an isolated house that sat between a lake and a wood. For two years the historian, writer and philosopher lived there, and the writing that came from the period is still prized today.

How did he enjoy it? Well, this might give some clue:

"This is a delicious evening, when the whole body is one sense and imbibes delight through every pore."

I'm not recommending we all find a cabin in the forest, but I do suggest we each find a place and a time when we can simply be, away from the world and its demands, and soak up the delight of that feeling. Ahhh.

Sunday — October 27

LINDA is a poet who writes in Tuscany. Actually, she lives and writes in Scotland, but she loves Tuscany and finds it the most inspiring place ever. So, she decorated the inside of her garden shed with a Tuscan rug and tapestry. Tuscan ornaments and dried flowers adorn her shelves and a Tuscan candle sits by her laptop.

Even on a dreich Scottish day Linda can still be in Tuscany.

Similarly, we might long for Heaven even though it is currently out of reach. But there's nothing to stop us bringing as much of it as possible into our everyday lives.

Monday — October 28

THE Lady of the House and I were discussing a couple we had met that morning. We felt they might become good friends in future.

"But it seemed different," I ventured. "Not like meeting up with any of our usual crew."

"Ah," she said. "It's because they're new, that's all. The "usual crew", as you call them, have been with us long enough for us to be comfortable with them. Which doesn't make them any less important. In fact, I'd say we need old friends to grow old with, and new friends to keep us young."

That's what the strange feeling was! Youth!

Tuesday — October 29

IT sounds like a profound truth from a religious text. "If we should deal out justice only in this world, who would escape? No, it is better to be generous and, in the end, more profitable. It gains gratitude for us, and love."

If those words were spoken by some divine being we might appreciate them, but feel justified in failing to live up to them. After all, we are not divine. But they were written by Mark Twain.

And, if a man can think of them, surely the rest of us can live them.

Wednesday — October 30

IT'S a rare group, or family, or community, where everyone likes everyone and everyone gets on. So, what do you do when you find yourself in a gathering with that one person?

I know we are expected to make the effort, but why can't we just do what is best for us instead of always having to do the right thing? Actually, as usual, they are the same thing.

We could walk away, ignore them, be snooty. But anyone could do that. And most people would do it, because it's the easy thing to do.

Speaking to someone when you don't want to? Being pleasant to someone who isn't? Turning animosity into friendship? That's so difficult that most people would rather not try. Then they blame it on the other person.

You could do that. Or you could do the right thing. The difficult thing. Overcoming your doubts, animosity and the challenge.

The group will be better off. The other individual might (or might not) appreciate it. But you will be a better person because of it!

Thursday — October 31

I HAPPENED to be in Bristol when I saw the little child. She had armfuls of teddies and dollies, each of which she was prepared to drop before letting go of her blanket. Her comfort and security were in that woven square.

Legend has it that, in the 14th century, Thomas Blanket of Bristol came up with the idea of weaving wool with a raised knap to make a warmer night-covering after he and his wife became tired of shivering in bed.

He then set up a manufactory which soon gained the approval and protection of the King. Perhaps the King also appreciated being cosy at night.

No doubt it made Mr Blanket's fame and fortune, but he could never have imagined his new process would bring such reassurance to generations of children as they toddle about, security blanket in hand.

November

Friday — November 1

THE Japanese term *ichi-go, ichi-e* means "one-time, one-meeting". It's a lovely reminder that each moment, each encounter, is unique and will never be repeated. We might meet a friend in the same place two days in a row, but we will be different people, bearing another day's worth of worries or delights.

The river we step in one moment will be just as wet the next time we do it, but it won't be the same water. The sun rises every morning, but we see it through different clouds and in different skies.

Ichi-go, ichi-e. This moment will never happen again. Treasure it!

Saturday — November 2

ALISON sat on a rock by the sea. It was the day of her friend's funeral, but she was thousands of miles away. So, she bought a mixed bouquet and, dedicating each flower to an aspect of their friendship, she offered them to the waves.

One was for support, one for the confidences shared, one for the laughter . . . and so on.

The last flower, which happened to be a rose, Alison decided was simply for her friend. And in it went.

But, a moment later, a wave brought it back. She threw it in again. It came back again. And a third time.

So she dried it with a tissue and took it home.

That was seven years ago. Showing me the rose pressed into her scrap-book and telling me about it, Alison asked if I knew what that meant.

I had a feeling I did, but I let her complete the story.

"Friends never really leave you," she said.

River deep, mountain high.

River Wye, Wales.

Sunday — November 3

IF you want to know more about the Apostle Thomas than the "Doubting Thomas" story, you could try reading the apocryphal gospel that bears his name. And you still wouldn't know any more about him!

That document is entirely composed of wisdom and sayings attributed to Jesus. In a way Thomas (if he actually wrote it) presents himself to posterity entirely through Jesus.

Not a bad legacy for a disciple – or any one of us!

Monday — November 4

TOOK my bike out of the garden shed. Then I threw it down on the grass. The gang were going exploring that day. A bike was a must but mine had a flat tyre. My day was wasted and I was not happy!"

I sipped my tea as I waited to hear more about ten-year-old Harry from his considerably more grown-up counterpart.

"Dad was watching from the kitchen window. He came out, handed me a puncture repair kit, and said, 'A flat tyre is like a bad attitude. You'll never get anywhere until you change it.'"

"And?"

"We had an amazing day, that day!"

Tuesday — November 5

DURING recent flooding, I saw an image that said so much about humanity. A baby was curled in its mother's arms, but the mother was cradled in the arms of a soldier who was part of the relief operation. He was taking them from a flooded home to a safe refuge.

The Army "carried", or supported, the soldier. He carried the woman. She carried the baby. All of that effort in support of innocence and helplessness.

People are wonderful, and never more so than when we carry each other.

Wednesday — November 6

WILLIAM LAMB, known as Lord Melbourne, was Prime Minister in 1834. History doesn't rate him as a great Prime Minister, noting instead that he presided over a calm period in British history. He fought no great battles, proclaimed no great philosophies.

Instead he carried on after the death of his son, reconciled with his wife after her infidelity, mentored and was a great help to the young Queen Victoria, and is remembered as "kind, honest and not self-seeking."

We could, perhaps, wish for a different understanding of history, and a different interpretation of what makes a man great.

Thursday — November 7

HAVE you ever felt like you wasted your time with someone? Perhaps they left you feeling the money you spent on them was wasted, too. But what about the affection you gave?

The poet Henry Wadsworth Longfellow thought that had special qualities.

"Talk not of wasted affection," he wrote. "Affection was never wasted."

It will live on – in their hearts, in their minds – and, be reassured, it will do good!

Friday — November 8

ABRAHAM LINCOLN once said, "If we could first know where we are, and whither we are tending (heading), we could then better judge what to do and how to do it."

The thought is as applicable to our lives as it is to any problem needing a solution.

First, understand where you came from – the family, the place, the examples you learned from – then decide where you want to go in this life (and, perhaps, beyond that). Knowing those, you will have a better chance of planning your route, and judging your progress.

Saturday — November 9

OUT walking the dogs, I saw a hawk hovering above a field. Then, three crows attacked it from different directions. Working together, they could have given the hawk a rough time. But the bird of prey flew higher.

The crows regrouped and tried again. The hawk flew higher still. After one more try the crows gave up and went about their separate business. The hawk resumed its position, searching for lunch.

Walking on, I thought about the lesson Mother Nature had just shared with me. In times of trouble, rise above!

Sunday — November 10

HER laptop pinged, and a message popped up.
I see you. I love you!

It was from a friend, and just what she needed to hear at that moment. But, how?

Then she realised she was still logged into her online messaging system. It showed a little green light next to the pictures of any of her friends who were also online then. And a green light would be next to her picture on her friend's screen.

Such technology would have seemed magical not too long ago, but perhaps it brings us closer to believing that there is one who sees us, whether our light is shining bright or we are in the dark.

And He loves us, too.

Monday — November 11

A JUNIOR diplomat in the Paris peace talks after World War I, Harold Nicolson wrote, "We were preparing not peace only, but eternal peace. There was about us the halo of some divine mission."

Eternal peace was, sadly, not achieved then, but for the sake of all the victims of war the "divine mission" ought to go on. If enough of us made peace in our homes, it might spread to our neighbourhood, beyond that to our country, and beyond even that, to the world.

Tuesday — November 12

THE Lady of the House and I attended a large outdoor event. Taking our places among thousands of people filing through the security checks, I remarked on the pleasantness of all the event marshals we had encountered.

"Well, it's nice to be nice," the woman with the metal-detecting wand said. "But it's also part of the training. If we treat people like they might be trouble, then . . . But if we meet them with happiness and courtesy, we tend to get the same in return."

Oh, that more of us had the same training as we "event manage" our lives!

Wednesday — November 13

IT is, supposedly, an old Tibetan proverb – "The secret to living well and longer is: eat half, walk double, laugh triple and love without measure."

I'm not especially fussed about the living longer part of the equation. What will be, will be. But living well does appeal to me. And if we followed those suggestions – especially the last one – we would live a very full life, no matter how long it was!

Thursday — November 14

THE Tree of Life sits on a small cliff on the Washington State coast. "Sits" is probably the wrong word. From some angles, it seems to float.

The Sitka spruce grew above where a small stream was tunnelling its way to the sea. Eventually, all the earth under the tree fell away, but the tree stayed in place. Most of its roots are exposed and can do it little good, but it had spread them out far enough that it is attached to solid ground on three sides. The main body of the tree now floats, upright, over fresh air and is a popular visitor attraction.

When it comes to a good support system, be we human beings or a tree, it seems we can never spread ourselves too wide!

Friday — November 15

PLEASE keep me optimistic, Lord,
* When all the world looks grey;*
And plant new hope within my heart
Whatever comes my way.
Please help me count my blessings, too,
So many to be found,
And through each season of the year
Find beauty all around.

– Iris Hesselden.

Saturday — November 16

LOTS of people search for happiness – and lots don't! The latter group are usually too busy doing things to search for anything. They will generally be the happier group.

What they do doesn't matter; they might grow roses, collect stamps, compose music, write nursery rhymes, paint, climb hills or volunteer.

What matters is that they do it with a passion, they do it the best they can, and they find a purpose in it.

Happiness isn't found in the searching.

It is found in the doing.

Sunday — November 17

AS the nights get longer and the season darker, we might consider C.S. Lewis's explanation of why there must be a point to all of this.

"If the universe has no meaning," he wrote, "we should never have found out it had no meaning: just as, if there was no light in the universe and therefore no creatures with eyes, we should never know it was dark."

We know there is light because we also know the dark.

And we know there is meaning to the universe, because we were created in such a way as to wonder about it – or about Him.

Monday — November 18

PEOPLE often struggle with who they are supposed to be in this life. Some anonymous sage once suggested that we be the one we needed when we were younger.

Why? Well, I suppose that in becoming the person our younger self needed we will have felt the need, the worry, the fear, and become the solution to it.

We will be that good thing for others as well in our lives, of course, but we will also have filled a lack, completed a circle, and healed ourselves.

Tuesday — November 19

A CERTAIN town in Portugal has taken to hanging rows of brightly coloured umbrellas above its shopping areas during the hottest months of the year. Not only is it a bright and eye-catching art installation and tourist attraction, but it also serves a very useful function in keeping people cool.

Most of us will have an umbrella. And it will help keep us dry on wet days and perhaps shade us on sunny days. If we had 500 of them, they could do the same for 500 people. But if you tied those 500 together and hung them over a street, they would help thousands.

Working individually, we are OK. Working together, we are better!

Wednesday — November 20

HAVE you ever known two people to fall out because one felt they didn't get what they were owed from the other? It's a little thing, but it can have far-reaching consequences.

"If those who owe us nothing gave us nothing," the Italian-born Argentinian poet Antonio Porchia suggested, "how poor we would be!"

We might be slightly impoverished when those who owe us don't make that debt right, but we are enriched beyond measure by the gifts of those who owe us nothing.

Thursday — November 21

TRADEMARK infringement is a serious thing, and copyright law is big business these days. The students and staff at the college I visited probably knew all that. But that didn't stop one of them writing on the cafeteria white-board, "Your smile is your logo, your personality is your business card, and how you leave others feeling after they meet you is your trademark."

Those of us who aren't in business might still like to develop our own trademark.

Friday — November 22

THE sign proclaimed the name of the town we were coming into. Underneath it was the slogan, "Better than it has to be."

As slogans go, it didn't strike me as all that inspirational. Then I thought some more. There are so many expectations – social and legal – about how we ought to be, that normal good behaviour, while appreciated, is hardly surprising.

The real surprise comes when people (or places) exceed those expectations for no reason other than because they want to. Let's meet the world's expectations, and exceed them. Be better than we have to be. Just because we can!

Saturday — November 23

LIKE most ten-year-old boys, Craig doesn't have a clue about make-up. But his mother didn't think that was a good excuse for tormenting his older sister while she applied her powder and paint.

"But, Mum, she made such a funny face!" he protested.

Mum discovered the sixteen-year-old had been trying to hold a big smile while doing her face. She had read somewhere that this was the best way to apply make-up to maximum effect. And that was what her brother had found so entertaining.

After Mum had smoothed everyone's ruffled feathers, she assured her children that smiling didn't just bring out the best in make-up – it was the best way to get "maximum effect" from life as well!

A new day dawns.

Chrome Hill, Peak District, England.

Sunday — November 24

THE other man stormed off, leaving Harry looking annoyed, but thoughtful.

"Well," I said, having caught the end of their heated discussion. "You won't be talking to him again, will you?"

"If I have learned anything in all my years," Harry said, "it's that the ones who put on the hardest fronts are the ones who most want to be appreciated and understood. I will talk to him again – when I can figure out a good way to do one or other of those things."

I said nothing. I had nothing to offer that compared with such wisdom. I'm sure Harry understood.

Monday — November 25

TAKE the time to look around you,
Even on a busy day,
Special moments are important
As you travel on life's way.
Notice how the trees are changing,
Every season something new,
Distant hills, now clear, now misty,
Every day a different view.

– Iris Hesselden.

Tuesday — November 26

E. JOSEPH COSSMAN was an American salesman who made his millions through mass-marketing novelties, such as ant-farms and spud-guns. He once said, "If you want to test your memory, try to recall what you were worrying about one year ago today."

Of course, that's not so much a test of your memory as a test of how important, or unimportant, the things you were worrying about really were.

With that in mind, the thing that's worrying you now, do you think you'll be able to recall it in a year? Even with a good memory?

Wednesday — November 27

DID you ever get told off as a child (or, perhaps, as an adult) for living in a fantasy world? I do hope so!

Maya Angelou wrote, "If one is lucky, a solitary fantasy can totally transform one million realities."

Of course, it all depends on what the fantasy is. For many, the notions that this is a wonderful world and that people are inherently kind are fantasies. They often make a good case for their argument – not that I tend to believe them.

And it never seems to occur to them that their reality actually makes the world a poorer place.

But, the more we live as if good fantasies are true, the more they tend to become true (or be revealed as actual truths), the more they encourage other examples to pop up, the more people are likely to join us in our "fantasy".

Then it might just be the cynic's harsh reality that turns out to be the fantasy after all.

Thursday — November 28

MANY American traditions began in the various European countries the early settlers came from. And some of the newer ones have, in turn, found their way back to our shores. Thanksgiving Day might never catch on here, though, because it specifically commemorates the time the early settlers were saved from starvation by the natives of the land they were so unfamiliar with. If it hadn't been for the help offered at that time the United States as we know them now might never have come to be.

But a day dedicated to giving thanks is never a bad idea, wherever in the world we might live.

As our American friends celebrate with family, food and football, the rest of us might give a little thought to thanksgiving.

An American, the minister and educator Henry van Dyke, long ago provided us with a perfect definition of it.

"Gratitude," he wrote, "is the inward feeling of kindness received. Thankfulness is the natural impulse to express that feeling."

Friday — November 29

THERE'S a story of two boys walking by a cliff-edge. A stag came bounding towards them, looking frantically for an escape route. He considered jumping into the sea, then swept around and headed for nearby trees.

The boys knew the approaching hunters would ask which way their prey went. They could tell them he went into the water and the hunt would be called off, but they would be lying. Or they could answer truthfully and risk him being caught.

The moment came and the hunt-master asked the question.

"Play fair! And it's not fair to ask us. We're on his side!" one of the boys blurted out.

In matters of conscience, when you are not sure what to say, declare your side. And make it a side you can be proud of.

Saturday — November 30

WE planned to treat some young friends to a few rides at the fun-fair, but the Lady of the House and I arrived a little early.

The fun-fair was set up, partly, on a high riverbank. Walking around the trucks, the caravans, the inflatables and everything that twisted, swung and twirled high in the air, we found a bench and decided to sit there a while. With generators thundering behind us, and all the noise of the fair beyond that, we took in the view of the river.

Water tumbled over a weir, a heron watched from the river-bend, white clouds sailed across the sky, and an island could be seen off the coast.

My sweetheart rested her head on my shoulder. I laid my cheek against her hair and we all but drifted away in the peace. Until, that is, our excited young friends spotted us and came running over!

But, if nothing else, it showed me that heavenly peace can be found even in the noisiest of places.

December

CASTROL isn't his given name. It's what he's called by friends. It's the brand-name of a car engine oil .

"Castrol's the kind of guy for who, when he's around, things just go more smoothly and there's rarely any friction," his friend explained. "If he's not around, things tend to seize up and grind to a halt."

Barnabas was a similar type of man. When the disciples needed troublesome Saul of Tarsus to be brought into the fold they sent the "son of encouragement". When Paul fell out with John Mark, Barnabas healed the rift. As a result, we have the Gospel of Mark.

There are plenty of people in the world who will put up road-blocks and bring things to a stop. We need more of those who will speak the encouraging word, those who will keep things running smoothly.

We need more Barnabases – and Castrols!

THE children ran upstairs, excited to be on a double-decker bus. Two boys grabbed the front seats and the two girls sat behind them. They talked and laughed, jumping up when the sea came into view, got really excited when the bus approached a level-crossing, and stared open-mouthed as a train crossed the road.

Then they started singing a nursery song I recognised. Well, I recognised the tune, but the words were in a foreign language. And their clothing suggested this was not their first home. Perhaps they were refugees, or here for some other reason. But, change the clothes and the language and they could have been children from anywhere.

Wouldn't it be interesting if us grown-ups focused more on the many things we have in common, rather than the few things that keep us apart?

Tuesday — December 3

WE were having breakfast in the café, talking about givers and takers, when our friend Mary said, "There are three different types of givers, Francis. Rocks, sponges and honeycombs."

I thanked the waitress, then said, "Tell me."

"To get anything from a rock," she said, "you need to hit it with a hammer. And what you get is mostly noise and sparks. A sponge will give you plenty but you need to squeeze it first. And the honeycomb? Well, it just naturally overflows with its own sweetness."

"Ha! And which are you?" I asked.

"I'm too busy to answer that. I must buzz." Mary added a spoonful of honey to my porridge and off she went, a busy little bee who knows all she needs to know about giving.

Wednesday — December 4

I WAS in a hospital chapel – or spiritual area – earlier. There was a little alcove where a notepad lay open. A sign told visitors that prayers written down would be respectfully raised before God.

I took two attempts to read through that book, and turned away in tears each time. There were hopes for successful outcomes, thanks for peaceful departures. One just said, "I thank you, I thank you, I thank you! Amen!" One told how they had just met someone who was severely depressed after a particularly serious diagnosis. They were able to tell the person that they had lived with the same condition for twenty-five years, so far.

The words Dad, Mum, son, daughter, husband and wife almost crackled on the pages from the love they contained.

As I left the chapel, I looked down the corridor, at patients, staff, visitors. They probably weren't the people who wrote those prayers, but they were living similar lives, full of experiences that might overwhelm some, confuse others, lift some up to a higher place.

We treat each other so casually at times, but if we could really know people's prayers, how could we help but love each other?

Thursday — December 5

BOHUN LYNCH was a prolific writer in the early 1900s. He wrote on boxing, created science fiction adventures, compiled a volume of letters from the South Seas, published collections of ghost stories, and so on.

His very last book was called "The Perfect Day" and, in one way or another, that was just what his fictional hero had, even down to taking delight in the feel, sound and smell of a new box of matches.

Live this day (and the next) appreciating the little things. It's the best way to make every day a perfect day.

Friday — December 6

THERE'S no point in it," he said.
"I don't care. I think it's beautiful."

"You're a fool, then," he replied, and off he walked.

Was he right? Was I? Who knows. We had shared the same experience. But we saw it differently and who is to judge whether one opinion is better than another?

So, is there any point to all of this? Only that I was happy and he wasn't. In a world where one view carries as much weight as the next one, we might as well choose the one that makes us happy.

Saturday — December 7

DECEMBER isn't typically thought of as a gardening month, although it is said that the garden season begins on January 1 and ends December 31. Katharine White, magazine editor and wife of E.B. White who wrote "Charlotte's Web", was a keen gardener and, in her own way, she didn't stop.

"From December to March," she wrote, "there are, for many of us, three gardens – the garden outdoors, the garden of pots and bowls in the house, and the garden of the mind's eye."

That last one is a garden we can all enjoy, at any time of year!

A miniature work of art.

Sunday — December 8

*WHEN the miracle happened it was not
With bright light or fire,
But a farm door
With the thick smell of sheep
And wind tugging at the shutters.*

*There was no sign the world had changed for ever
Or that God had taken place;
Just a child crying softly in a corner,
And the door left open,
For those who came to find.*

– Kenneth Steven.

Monday — December 9

A JAPANESE fable tells of a nobleman, a bonsai tree collector, in much reduced circumstances.

In the midst of a harsh winter he receives a travelling monk, but regrets he has no fire to warm him by. Then he remembers the remnants of his once fine bonsai collection: a little plum tree, a little cherry tree and a little pine tree.

It grieves him sorely, but he kindles a fire, and warms the traveller.

Only, it turns out that the "monk" is a Shogun in disguise. The Shogun gifts the man three parcels of land, calling them Plumland, Cherryland and Pineland.

The Bible tells us that in being hospitable to a stranger, some have entertained angels.

In this case it was a powerful ruler. But, even if the stranger is really just an ordinary traveller, you will have helped a soul like your own travel a little further along the difficult road that life can sometimes be.

That's a beautiful thing in its own right, and reward enough for most.

Tuesday — December 10

FLANNERY O'CONNOR, the American novelist, never wrote directly about faith, but her characters frequently had to deal with matters of religion as they affected their everyday lives.

A character of hers once spoke a line that surely came from Ms O'Connor's own attitude. It was "I can, with one eye squinted, take it all as a blessing."

Whether everything in life is a blessing or not is surely a decision taken long ago and up above. All we get to decide is whether we see them or not. Sometimes it's obvious, but sometimes we need to squint a little!

Wednesday — December 11

A PHOTOGRAPHER wanted to capture the spirit of a festival, but every time she asked to take a picture the person "put a face on". It was nice, but not really genuine. So then she started asking people if she could thank them – male, female, and all races and ages – with a kiss! Then she took a second photo.

The second photos were happier, more vibrant, somehow more like the authentic person.

There is more to almost everyone we meet. The trick is to find a way beyond the public face they (and we) wear. But, if kissing them is your chosen technique, be sure to ask first!

Thursday — December 12

WRITING of a friend from days gone by, J.B. Priestley said, "He was no fool – except in the way that all really nice people are fools."

A bit harsh? Perhaps, but not so far off the mark as far as I am concerned.

Really nice people are generally open and vulnerable enough that they could be taken for a fool, if anyone had a mind to. But that same openness and vulnerability is generally what brings out the best in us, ensuring we would never do such a thing!

Friday — December 13

MARCUS AURELIUS was a man of great power, but that was not what he longed to be. He knew the empire he ruled might be taken from him by force, or by intrigue. He might be killed, or exiled. All of these things might happen to him at the hands of others.

But his ultimate goal could be taken from him by no man.

"For who is he," the Emperor wrote, "that shall hinder thee from being good and simple?"

No-one can give us those qualities. We may have to work at them. But, having achieved them, no-one can take them from us.

Saturday — December 14

SHE asked me the secret of my happiness, assuring me she had asked others the same but received no satisfactory answer. I asked her who she had asked, and I was surprised.

When I told her I had often known these individuals to be otherwise she insisted she had always known them to be very happy people – in her company. And there was the secret of happiness, of their happiness, at least. It was her.

And I had a new question for her: would she rather be happy, as they were, or be the one who brings out the happiness in everyone around her?

Sunday — December 15

SINGER and radio presenter "King" Coleman fronted a regular six-hour, faith-based radio show called "Nothing But Love" until his recent death.

I doubt if all the songs he played were about love, but I don't doubt that he loved God and music. The programme was how he shared that with his listeners.

We can't all be radio presenters, but we might try to find some other way of sharing our experience of God.

If we do it properly then it, too, will be nothing but love.

Monday — December 16

SIDONIE-GABRIELLE COLETTE (known as Colette) was a French novelist. She wrote the book that went on to become the musical "Gigi". She was nominated for a Nobel Prize in literature. She was a mime artist and a journalist. She also had a secret for staying young!

"You must not pity me," she wrote, "because my sixtieth year finds me still astonished. To be astonished is one of the surest ways of not growing old too quickly."

I'm astonished she said that! Just in case she was right.

Tuesday — December 17

THE title of Joseph Conrad's novel "Heart Of Darkness" refers to a journey into unexplored territory in the "Dark Continent", Africa. It also refers to the apparent madness of one of his characters. No doubt it's a fine read and a thought-provoking novel.

Another example of a heart of darkness appeals to me more. Referring to times of grief or loss, the French novelist Jean Giraudoux wrote, "Sadness flies on the wings of the morning and out of the heart of darkness comes the light."

The light is always in there, no matter how well we cover it up!

Wednesday — December 18

THERE used to be a saying in Siberia that, in the coldest part of the winter, a person's words could freeze in the air before falling into the snow. Then, come spring, the words would thaw out and people passing by might hear those defrosted snatches of speech whispering back into the air. What an amazing phenomenon if it were true!

What is true is that in the "winter" of our anger we might say something that stays frozen in another's heart and comes back to haunt us at happier times.

The seasons change, disputes melt away. Rather than speaking words that might chill a summer's day, perhaps we should focus on words that warm the winter. One thing is for sure, we will never regret speaking them.

A capital sight.

Jubilee Gardens and Westminster Palace, London.

Thursday — December 19

EVERYONE will tell you it is better to forgive than to keep on holding a grudge. And we, in our hurt, often respond by saying that they don't understand how difficult that is.

But we rarely stop to think how much more difficult holding a grudge can be. It means we need to remember whatever offended us, for ever. It means we need to spoil any number of good days with the memory. For ever.

It means we need to have our avoiding techniques, or retaliatory actions, all lined up and ready to spring into action when the other person appears. For ever.

Now, it's possible we might convince ourselves that whatever the other person did actually deserves all of that unpleasantness. But what did you and I do to deserve having it in our lives, for ever? Forgiveness doesn't just benefit the other person (if, in fact, they accept it as a benefit). Your future self will thank you.

Friday — December 20

THE Lady of the House sighed. Then she sighed again. I took my cue, asked if she was OK.

She came over to my desk to show me a picture of a dress she had had her eye on for some time.

"I just love it," she said. "But I can't imagine I would ever have a suitable occasion to wear it."

Making it seem like a casual remark, but having weighed up all the options – including the unappetising prospect of getting gussied up myself – I spoke.

"Buy the dress. We'll make an occasion."

It was more than me simply keeping my better half sweet, though. You see, the dress was gorgeous, and she would bring out the best in it. But I believe we ought to do more than simply appreciate the beauty in front of us. Sometimes we need to play our part in creating it.

So, now I'm in search of an occasion for my sweetheart to shine at. If you hear of any . . .

Saturday — December 21

I HAVE friends who are brothers and yet have very different outlooks on life. One is the eternal optimist, the other thinks his brother foolish because there is so much wrong with this world. But, as much as he finds that is wrong, his brother finds as much that is right.

The world is not a wonderful place – and yet it is.

The world is not harsh and difficult – and yet it is.

The sensible way, it seems to me, is to accept that this is a world of contradictions and no one view of it is the correct one.

Having said that, having accepted that, the only sensible question that remains is, which of these opposing views will we live in, which will we hold closest to us?

Young Anne Frank's family were probably hiding from the Nazis in fear for their lives, and would have had plenty of reasons for looking on the dark side, when she wrote, "I don't think of all the misery – but of the beauty that still remains."

Even the most hardened cynic could not argue with the fact that, despite everything, there is much that is beautiful. Let's focus on that. And in doing so, I believe we will discover more beauty than we could ever have imagined.

Sunday — December 22

BOB doesn't subscribe to any of the online movie channels, like Netflix or Amazon. But, last Christmas, he gifted his daughter a subscription so his granddaughter could watch the cartoons.

Recently, five-year-old Evie was telling him about the latest animations when she asked, "Do you have that channel, Gramps? You should. It's amazing!"

"It might or might not be amazing," Bob told me, "but it made me wonder. Evie has no idea the current delight of her life comes to her courtesy of her old Gramps – also known as someone who loves her.

"Perhaps, as someone who ought to know better, I should pay more attention to the things in my life provided by those who love me, from the ones who love me at home to the One who came down at Christmas to love us all."

Monday — December 23

I DON'T think anyone would deny there is a special feeling at Christmas-time. If we celebrate with gifts or with none, with family or alone, anyone who is out and about over these next few days can't help but be aware that something special is happening.

The preacher and writer Dr Norman Vincent Peale described it like this: "Christmas waves a magic wand over the world and behold, everything is softer and more beautiful."

Tuesday — December 24

C HRISTMAS carols, or festive songs, might be based on fancy, forgotten traditions, or faith. Good King Wenceslas stands out from the others in that it is actually about a real human being. He was a duke rather than a king, but the song got the other detail right: he really was good!

As a Christian in a pagan family he tried to live the faith in the most practical ways. He regularly fed the hungry, and the notion of him taking firewood to the poor in the depths of winter fits right in with what is known about him.

Unfortunately, the world he lived in was not as kind as his heart was. He was killed in a power struggle before he had time to grow old, but the ordinary people remembered him with love – even to the extent of singing about him.

In the song, a page-boy follows in his footsteps, and is warmed by them. But Wenceslas would never have thought of himself as the example to be followed. He was following a higher example, and learning as he did so.

If we would be a force for good in this world, we might be inspired by the deeds of others, but when we look for an example, we might as well choose the best. Walk in the footsteps of the One whose footsteps Good King Wenceslas followed.

The page-boy felt warmed in the snow by following his Duke. What wonders might we experience, walking behind the King of Peace and Love?

Wednesday — December 25

A CHILD, on hearing Santa had a Naughty and Nice List, asked what would happen if the naughty children outnumbered the others. Would Santa stay at home? I confidently assured her it would never happen. Despite all that is wrong with this world, I firmly believe there is, and always will be, more that is good and pure.

And, even if it did happen, the One whose birth we celebrate today brought gifts, too big for Santa's sack, for all of us no matter which list we are on.

Love. And forgiveness.

Thursday — December 26

HAVE you heard of the Christmas spider? A Ukrainian tradition tells of a woman too poor to decorate her Christmas tree. This upset her. So, while she was in bed, God sent a spider to decorate her tree with its web.

I know, I know. Many would take a broom to it.

But, imagine how that fine silken craft-work would have looked in the morning's light!

We'll all have decorated our trees and our homes by now, if we had the money to do so. And I'm sure they look lovely, but, in the quiet time between Christmas and New Year, take the chance to enjoy the beauty we get for free: the silence, the wind in the trees, a crisp starry evening, laughter, sunsets.

Spider-webs, if you will.

And I hope your gifts will have been well given and well received, but as you appreciate the beauty we have for free, think a while on the gifts we take for granted, like friends and family, love, health if we have it, each new day bringing the chance of a fresh start, and so on.

If, among all the hustle and bustle, we give thanks for all we have through grace, we will be closer to the spirit of Christmas than we might realise.

Friday — December 27

"OH, Christmas was all about hymns and prayer." Morag recalled her childhood in a shepherd's cottage. "There were no gifts."

Perhaps, but family gathered from miles around and they stayed the week, or until the weather allowed them to leave.

And a pig was butchered, and some home-brewed drink was shared, and children shared crowded beds, and there were many dogs chasing the scraps under a well-laden table, and memories were shared, and dreams were discussed.

Hymns and prayer may have been what those Christmases were all about, but the whole occasion sounds like a gift to me.

Saturday — December 28

AT this time of year, I often find myself out under black, star-speckled skies. I miss the lighter evenings and warmer times of summer, just like I miss the easy movements and the spring my steps used to have in younger years. But I also enjoy a clear winter's night and appreciate the storehouse of memories experience brings.

Thankfully, we don't have to choose one or the other. With God's grace, we get both.

The poet Henry Wadsworth Longfellow may have been thinking something similar when he wrote, "For age is opportunity, no less than youth itself, though in another dress. And as the evening twilight fades away, the sky is filled with stars, invisible by day."

Sunday — December 29

IN her novel "Their Eyes Were Watching God", about growing up in a racially segregated community, Zora Hurston wrote, "Some people could look at a mud puddle and see an ocean with sailing ships."

If we look at the world as a creation of His, an interconnected, intricately planned miracle, it is difficult for us to see anything as ordinary.

It isn't always easy to see things that way, but this season has no shortage of muddy puddles, so we might as well give it a try.

THE awe-struck shepherds in the night
Saw hordes of angels singing,
And all the bells in heaven above
Were jubilantly ringing.
But in that stable all is calm
On this first Christmas morn,
And Mary finally can rest
Now that her child is born.
They've travelled many weary miles
In misery and cold,
She knows she's borne the Son of God
As the angel had foretold.
She does not know that she will face
The agony and loss
Of seeing her own beloved son
Die on a Calvary cross.
So let her cradle her sweet babe
With love so strong and deep,
May blessed peace surround her now
And let poor Mary sleep.

– Eileen Hay.

IN the classic caricature of the tramp, he usually carries all his worldly goods in a "bundle" – a square piece of cloth with all the corners tied together and hoisted over his shoulder on a stick.

In his poem "Open The Door", Scots poet William Soutar suggests we "bundle" up the worries of the past twelve months and let the old year take them with him as he tramps into the past.

"Open your hert for the new life. And let the bairn come in." The bairn is the new year, waiting to journey into the future with us.

Children (bairns), whether actual or metaphorical, ought always to bring joy and possibilities with them as their gifts to the world. May the year to come be, to you and yours, a time of opened hearts, new life, new loves and new joys!

A chilly family outing.